C000096887

For your reading pleasure

CORNWALL'S
STRANGEST
TALES

For your reading pleasure

CORNWALL'S STRANGEST TALES

EXTRAORDINARY BUT TRUE STORIES

A VERY CURIOUS HISTORY

PETER GREGO

PORTICO

First published in the United Kingdom in 2013 by
Portico Books
10 Southcombe Street
London
W14 0RA

An imprint of Anova Books Company Ltd

Copyright © Portico Books, 2013

All rights reserved. No part of this publication may be reproduced,
stored in a retrieval system, or transmitted in any form or by any
means electronic, mechanical, photocopying, recording or otherwise,
without the prior written permission of the copyright owner.

ISBN 9781909396005

A CIP catalogue record for this book is available from the British Library.

10 9 8 7 6 5 4 3 2 1

Printed and bound by Bookwell, Finland

This book can be ordered direct from the publisher at
www.anovabooks.com

CONTENTS

INTRODUCTION

Childhood summer holidays in the Southwest during the 1970s are among my most precious memories. The back seat of Dad's Morris Traveller always seemed to be a safe, comfortable spot from which to view, admire, absorb and mentally elaborate on the passing scenery. Thinking back to those days, it's surprising that daydreams and romantic fancies managed to manifest themselves at all in the mind of a child whose nose was occasionally pressed yet harder against the side window by bouts of bickering among his older brother and two younger sisters beside him. Yet the cramped, often turbulent confines of that half-timbered car were, somehow, successfully escaped from in our excursions through Somerset, Devon and Cornwall.

Even at an early age I had the impression that Cornwall was a different kind of English county. Cornwall seemed older and in some ways harsher, held closer to the whims of nature. Not only was it patently different from my home in Birmingham (which in 1974 was excised from Warwickshire to become part of the new, grey county of the industrial West Midlands), but also obviously different from the rude rural cheese-and-scrumpiness of Somerset and the cosy clotted-creaminess of Devon. My mind formed no such quaint general template whenever Cornwall was pondered; tin miners, bleak moorlands, china clay pyramids, fishing boats and fabulous surfs vied for attention. Whatever Cornwall was, it was a place of contrasts as varied as its daily weather; generalisation seemed futile. I now live in Cornwall, and I still have those same feelings.

Renowned for works featuring his native Dorset, Victorian novelist and poet Thomas Hardy (1840–1928) was deeply moved by Cornwall on his first visit to the county, writing that 'the place is pre-eminently the region of dream and mystery'. That's no mean compliment from one whose imagination and creativity ranged far and wide. It's no exaggeration to claim that such an impression of Cornwall has been felt — not only by writers and artists, but by everyone who has an eye for beauty and a sense of the ethereal — throughout the centuries. It's an impression that remains potent, capable of striking the visitor to 21st-century Cornwall with just as much force.

In showcasing a wide range of tales of strangeness and mystery this book intends to kindle the flames of the imagination without sacrificing objectivity or hijacking the reader's credulity. Some of our forays into weirdness are obviously misty folklore, misinterpretations of nature and journeys of anecdote; others, grounded in fact, are just as capable of inducing surprise, amazement and awe.

A DEARTH OF DINOSAURS
363,000,000 BC

Not so long ago, Cornwall was a tropical paradise consisting of a group of sunbathed islands surrounded by coral reefs and an abundance of exotic marine creatures. Of course, my reference to the recent nature of this scenario is in comparison with geological time. 'Not so long ago' is several hundred million years as compared with the several billion years that the Earth has existed. Maybe you're inclined to doubt the firm scientific evidence for this picture? In that case, perhaps you'd rather visit the Creation Science Centre in Cornwall, Ontario, where the friendly guides will tell you that the Earth is just 6,000 years old and fossils are the unfortunates who fell victim to Noah's flood (or were planted there as a 'test of faith').

Cornwall is no great friend to the fossil hunter. Comprised mostly of old, unfossiliferous rocks of igneous and metamorphic origin, the county can boast of no 'Jurassic Coast' where the evidence of weird and wonderful life forms from bygone epochs fall out of the cliff faces into the hands of delighted palaeontologists below. Although most examples of the fossils to be found in Cornwall are usually poorly preserved and the pickings are slim indeed, the dedicated fossil hunter may find some consolation in the fact that any ancient life to be alighted upon is *really* ancient.

From a geological perspective, Cornwall is extremely interesting. The Carboniferous Period, 363 to 290 million years ago, saw the county (or the place that would later form its bedrocks) deep below a narrow sea between the northern continent of Laurasia (Caledonia) and the southern plate of Normania. As Normania pushed northwards, the tract of sea was slowly being squeezed into ever-more narrow a space, producing islands surrounded by tropical seas, much like the Caribbean of today. These conditions favoured the deposition of limestone (calcium carbonate), a sedimentary rock made up of the skeletons of small plants and animals. Probably the best place to find fossils of the Lower Carboniferous are along Rusey Cliff (north Cornwall), where ancient corals, brachiopods (shells) and goniatites (broad, curling ammonites) can be found in a state of reasonable preservation. Upper Carboniferous fossils in sandstone, including fish remains and ancient worm burrows, can be found at Bude, Upton Cross and Widemouth Bay (also on the north coast). One fossil that many people prize in particular is the trilobite, a creature that was very successful in its time and which evolved into many weird and wonderful forms. California Quarry, an old cliff-top works, is strewn with grey slabs which contain two species of trilobite; whole forms are difficult to come by nowadays because of extensive fossil hunting, but parts of trilobites remain to be picked up.

As the Carboniferous sea silted over, Normania continued to muscle its way northwards. As a result, the oceanic crust was buckled up in its path, forming an extremely rare example where rocks usually only found in the mantle, deep beneath the crust, are visible today at the Earth's surface. The southern point of the Lizard displays such rocks, known as serpentinites. California has adopted this rare material as its 'state rock'. Perhaps one day Cornwall might do so too?

CORNWALL'S DAYS OF ORE

c. 2000 BC

Although Cornwall is one of the most geographically isolated parts of Britain, paradoxically it appears to have enjoyed its fair share of visitors from across various parts of the ancient world. Visitors from Ancient Egypt, Phoenicia, Greece and Rome have at various times trodden Cornish soil and interacted with the natives.

Cornwall's popularity in those far-off days was hardly attributable to its spectacular scenery, stretches of golden sands or board-rideable surfs. Cornwall had something far more precious – tin and copper (in addition to other valuable ores) found near the Earth's surface and running through its very bedrock. Such easily mined resources were pretty scarce in other parts of Europe.

What made these metals so special? Around 5,000 years ago the Sumerians discovered that a small amount of tin ore added to molten copper produced an incredible new alloy – bronze. Bronze was harder than tin or copper but was far easier to fashion (by means of casting) into useful things like weapons, armour, agricultural implements, household objects and jewellery. So ended the Stone Age, and with the Bronze Age came a growing international interest in Cornwall. The county's metal resources began to be exploited around 4,000 years ago with the burgeoning demands of the civilisations of the Near East and Europe. Prosperity increased and early Bronze Age settlements sprang up around the county, some of whose remains still exist in places.

Two particularly beautiful archaeological artefacts – a fine gold cup and a bronze sword hilt – illustrate the connection between ancient Mediterranean cultures and Cornwall. A sensation was caused in 1837 when archaeologists excavating Rillaton Barrow (on eastern Bodmin Moor near Liskeard) unearthed a fabulous gold cup. The ancient burial with which it is associated, along with other grave goods, indicates that the object was owned by a person of very high ranking, probably a chieftain or royal family member. Having been cleaned and restored it served for a while in the ignominious role as a holder for King George V's collar studs; thankfully the Rillaton Gold Cup can now be seen in the British Museum. It displays remarkably adept Aegean-style metalwork and is thought to have been made around 2,300 BC. Strangely enough, a local legend claimed that a mysterious gold cup lay deep within the barrow – could this possibly have been a memory passed down through a couple of hundred local generations? Another example of an Aegean import, probably Mycenaean, is the so-called Pelynt Dagger – actually an ornate bronze sword hilt – found in 1845 in Pelynt Barrow near Looe and now on display at the Royal Cornwall Museum, Truro.

Bronze Age Cornish prosperity peaked at around 1,500 BC, followed by a social decline. The Celts had begun to populate parts of Europe and the British Isles, introducing new farming practices and communities that were more geared to martial matters. While it's not known whether there was a violent clash of cultures between the ancient inhabitants of Cornwall and the Celts, it is certain that the seafaring Veneti, Celts of the Brittany peninsula, managed to seize control of the metal trade between Cornwall and the rest of Europe. Around 1,000 BC there was a sudden resurgence in metalcraft and more technologically sophisticated design.

But the magic and usefulness of bronze began to evaporate in the 8th century BC when the Iron Age arrived in Britain. Iron ore is smelted, cast into ingots and hammer-fashioned into implements by blacksmiths; with the addition of carbon it becomes steel, a material weighing about the same as bronze but far harder and more suited to weaponry and agriculture. With its acidic soil, Cornwall has few surviving iron implements from this era, and the patchy nature of human settlement in the county has made it difficult to identify sites linked with iron working. One of the few examples lies at Trevelgue Head Iron Age settlement on the cliffs above Newquay, where the remnants of an ancient foundry have been unearthed.

Cornwall continued to mine and export its metals, whose uses changed with technological advances, right up to modern times. With the closure of South Crofty near the village of Pool in 1998 came an end to four thousand years of Cornish metal mining – for the time being, at least, for the story of Cornwall's metal wealth may not yet be finished.

THE FIRST TOURIST IN CORNWALL

c. 325 BC

Around 325 BC the geographer Pytheas set out from his home in the Greek colony of Massalia (modern-day Marseilles) to explore the northern coasts of Europe and the mainland of Great Britain. In addition to expanding his knowledge of what was then virtually unknown territory, he was most probably seeking commercial sources of precious materials such as tin and amber. Sadly, Pytheas' account of his travels, *On the Ocean*, hasn't survived intact, but passages from it and references to it are to be found in the works of others, such as *Historical Library* (1st century BC) by the Greek historian Diodorus Siculus and *Natural History* (77 AD) by the Roman historian Pliny the Elder.

Relying on Pytheas as his source, Diodorus writes:

> Britain is triangular in shape...but its sides are not equal. This island stretches obliquely along the coast of Europe, and the point where it is least distant from the mainland, we are told, is the promontory which men call Cantium [Kent]...whereas the second promontory, known as Belerium [the Penwith peninsula of Cornwall], is said to be a voyage of four days from the mainland, and the last, writers tell us, extends out into the open sea and is named Orca [the Orkneys]. Britain is inhabited by tribes which preserve in their ways of living the ancient manner of life. They use chariots in their wars...and their dwellings are humble, being built for the most part out of reeds or logs... As for their habits, they are simple...

After referring in less than flattering terms to the Cornish economy and weather (not much seems to have changed), he then details Cornish life:

> The inhabitants of Britain who dwell about the promontory known as Belerium [Cornwall] are especially hospitable to strangers and have adopted a civilised manner of life because of their intercourse with merchants of other peoples. They it is who work the tin, treating the bed which bears it in an ingenious manner. This bed, being like rock, contains earthy seams and in them the workers quarry the ore, which they then melt down and cleanse of its impurities. Then they work the tin into pieces the size of knuckle-bones and convey it to an island which lies off Britain and is called Ictis [St Michael's Mount near Penzance]; for at the time of ebb-tide the space between this island and the mainland becomes dry and they can take the tin in large quantities over to the island on their wagons.

And from St Michael's Mount the tin would be purchased by merchants and distributed throughout Gaul and beyond. Whether Pytheas sampled an early Cornish pasty during his visit is unfortunately not recorded.

ANCIENT EARTHWORK
OF MYSTERY
c. 3RD CENTURY BC

'Near St Columb Major there is one of the most perfect remains of an ancient castle of the earthwork kind,' wrote the 'Cornish metaphysician' Samuel Drew in 1798. 'It is called Castle-an-Dinas, or, locally, King Arthur's Castle. It is enclosed by three rings of earth and stone, of which one was probably strengthened by a moat, and the inmost part covers an acre and a half.'

Constructed in the 3rd century BC, Castle-an-Dinas consists of three concentric ditches and mounds from whose domed centre, rising 150 feet above its surrounding landscape (685 feet above sea level), wonderful views can be had across the surrounding country to both north and south coasts. Archaeologists consider the structure to be one of the most impressive and important hillforts in the southwest. A part-excavation in the 1960s found two Bronze Age barrows within an area enclosed by the fort's circular ramparts, meaning that the site itself had been in use for centuries before the fort was built. Indeed, during more recent road construction the remains of a Stone Age settlement were discovered nearby.

During his visit to Cornwall in 1478, William of Worcester noted Castle-an-Dinas' legendary Arthurian connections. Legend says that Gorlois of Tintagel (Duke of Cornwall and first husband of Igraine, King Arthur's mother) was lured away to Castle-an-Dinas, where he died in battle, while Uther Pendragon, disguised as Gorlois with Merlin's help, slept with Igraine back at Tintagel. The amorous encounter led to King Arthur's conception. Samuel Drew himself claimed to have seen King Arthur's ghostly army above the area in 1798, and in 1867 Cornish cultural expert Henry Jenner heard an old man at nearby Quoit recalling how he had seen the ghosts of King

Arthur's soldiers drilling there. Jenner may have stifled a laugh as the man went on to remember how the moonbeams had glanced on the ancient Britons' muskets. The only time that Castle-an-Dinas is known to have been used for military purposes was in March 1645 during the English Civil War. A phalanx of Royalist troops led by Sir Ralph Hopton and retreating from defeat at Torrington camped there for two nights before surrendering to the Parliamentarians under Fairfax at Tresillian Bridge. Perhaps the old chap from Quoit had been confused; instead of King Arthur's men, had he witnessed the apparition of a group of frightened Cavaliers from around 200 years before?

Grisly murder has also reared its ugly head over Castle-an-Dinas. In June 1671 two young women, Anne Pollard and Loveday Rosebere, were found brutally murdered at the house of Captain Peter Pollard in St Columb. After setting a bloodhound on the trail, the murderer was found within a short space of time; local man John Trehenban's boots were covered in blood. He was sentenced to death by a most unusual means: imprisonment in a cage exposed atop Castle-an-Dinas. The rock upon which the death cage was anchored – a sizeable stone marked with an arrow – can still be seen.

In 1904 the body of Jessie Rickard, aged 18, was found by a group of youths lying in the outer ditch of Castle-an-Dinas. Police reported that she had been shot by a revolver in no less than six places: once in the left arm, once in the in the left cheek, twice by the left eye, once in the neck and once behind the left ear. Her lover, Charles Berryman, became chief suspect, but he evaded justice by skipping the country to the United States; his whereabouts were never discovered.

GONE AND ALMOST FORGOTTEN
6TH CENTURY AD

Penhale Sands – the immense sand dunes just north of Perranporth on the north coast of Cornwall – are a joy to climb, with superb views to be had over the bustling seaside town and the coast from on high. And beneath those sands lie the remains of the oldest Christian church in Britain.

Perranporth takes its name from the Cornish for 'cove of St Piran'. St Piran himself, one of Cornwall's patron saints, is thought to have come from Ireland in the 6th century, landing on Penhale Sands. Here in a hollow, St Piran built his tiny little church, fashioned in the Irish style with the heads of a man, a woman and a beast around the arched doorway. By the 10th century St Piran's Oratory had been abandoned because of the encroachment of sand. The site was excavated in 1835 and in 1910, but in the 1970s the remains of the stone building were left once more to nature. It now lies buried in the sand again. Nearby, an ancient eroded stone cross topped by a more recent granite stone and plaque can be found. It reads: 'This stone is dedicated to the glory of God and in memory of St. Piran, Irish missionary and Patron Saint of Tinners, who came to Cornwall in 6th Century. Beneath this stone is buried the Oratory which bears his name. Erected on the site hallowed by his prayers. October 1980'.

ANCIENT GRAFFITI
6TH CENTURY AD

It may consist only of three relatively small granite stones, but Men-an-Tol (Cornish: 'stone with a hole'), four miles northwest of Penzance, is perhaps Cornwall's most frequently pictured formation of standing stones. Forming a three-dimensional '101' shape, two upright stones, each three feet high, flank a round stone set on its edge with the centre holed out. It's not obvious, but there are other stones in the immediate vicinity, for the large part buried, which has led to the suggestion that it marks a now-vanished tomb or stone circle. It is entirely possible that the stones had an astronomical alignment, marking the rising points of the sun or moon at certain times of the year, with the hole and tips of the uprights forming a kind of sighting device. Few other ancient holed stones can be found in Cornwall – one, the Tolven Holed Stone, lies in a private garden near Helston, while another can be found at Zennor.

Myths and legends abound in connection with virtually every formation of standing stones, and Men-an-Tol is no exception. It has its own fairy guardian whose speciality is to effect miraculous cures. Legend has it that a changeling baby (the offspring of fairies secretly swapped for a human child) was passed through the holed stone; the stones did their trick and mother and original child were reunited. For obvious reasons, matters of fertility are especially relevant with Men-an-Tol. For centuries locals have claimed that a woman passing backwards through the holed stone seven times during full moon will find herself pregnant soon afterwards. Known to locals as the Crick Stone, it is said that crawling on all fours through the hole in a west-to-east direction will alleviate neck, back and other joint problems – although you might think it would make it worse! Another local legend tells that children will be cured of rickets when passed naked through the holed stone nine times.

Half a mile northwest of Men-an-Tol lies another ancient stone, the six-foot-high Men Scryfa (Cornish: 'inscribed stone'). Its inscription, made in the 6th century (more than a thousand years following its erection, making it perhaps the earliest example of graffiti in Cornwall), reads: *'Rialobrani Cunovali Filii'* (Latin for 'Rialobran, son of Cunoval'. In Cornish this translates into 'Royal Raven, son of the Glorious Prince'). We are meant to believe that the stone marks warrior Rialobran's burial place following his fatal wounding at the nearby battle of Gendhal Moor, a conflict so great that the 'streams ran with blood'. Legend has it that he merely sleeps beneath the stone, armed with his weapons and laden with treasures, ready to spring forth in Cornwall's hour of need.

WHAT'S IN A NAME?
891 AD

Strangely, there seems to be no general consensus concerning the origin of Cornwall's name. One of the more widely accepted theories is that it is a hybrid of separate terms from different languages. 'Corn-' is thought to come from the tribal name of the people who lived in the region since the Iron Age – the Cornovii. The Cornish word for Cornwall, 'Kernow', which dates from around 1400, seems to be derived from this tribal name. Old English provides the '-wall', from 'w(e)alh', meaning foreigner. Just taking the latter, the word 'Wales' shares the same root.

Cornovii itself (or Cornavii, Cornabii, and Curnavi) is thought to be a Roman reference to two or three British tribes – one based in Cornwall, part of the Dumnonii, another based in the Midlands and one in northern Scotland. Clearly, these were not one people. Cornovii, as related to the Cornish, may mean the 'people of the horn', possibly a reference to the tapering horn-shape of Cornwall. However, some have suggested that the tribe may have worshipped a horned deity, as did other tribes (including the Brigantes of northern England, with their horned god Cernunnos).

'On Corn Walum' – thought to be the earliest version of the word Cornwall – dates back to 891 AD, appearing in the Anglo-Saxon Chronicle. Two centuries later, things have changed a little towards the familiar – it was referred to as Cornualia in the Domesday Book. Another century later, it is referred to as the Duchy of Cornwal (one 'l').

TERRIFIC TINTAGEL
1233

Thirteenth-century Tintagel Castle, one of Cornwall's most distinctive and dramatic sites, sits in a commanding position upon a giant rounded promontory (virtually an island) at the mouth of a deep ravine that opens up onto the craggy north coast. It's a 'must visit' for the scenery alone, even if one chooses not to ascend the perilous-looking wooden steps that cling to the cliff face to explore the castle itself. Don't take my word for it – just take a look at J.M.W. Turner's 1818 portrayal of Tintagel Castle on display at Tate St Ives; the famous artist described how 'rocks on this part of the coast give rise to a great height, and present objects of awful contemplation'.

There's no evidence that Tintagel 'Island' was ever inhabited as a 'normal' community. The place has strong mythical associations with the legend of King Arthur and is reputed to have been the traditional seat of Cornish kings. 'Luxury items' – imported African pottery – found by archaeologists dating between the 5th and 8th centuries show that the place was very likely to have been used as an elite retreat for the great and good of Cornwall – the Dumnonian tribe who took over after the Romans left.

The castle itself, now a picturesque ruin, was constructed in 1233 by Richard, 1st Earl of Cornwall, to honour associations with ancient royalty and to firmly connect the place with King Arthur. But even in Richard's time, Arthur was but a distant legend. Later Earls of Cornwall neglected to maintain the castle and, being so exposed to the rough elements, it quickly fell into disrepair. A great revival of interest in Arthurian legend took place during the Victorian period, and curiosity about Tintagel surged. To promote tourism, the nearby village of Trevena changed its name to Tintagel. Although Tintagel Castle has such prominent ties with King Arthur, nowhere in the main source for the legend – Geoffrey of Monmouth's *History of the Kings of Britain* (1135) – does Arthur ever set foot there. Arthur's only link with the place seems to be that he was conceived there.

Tintagel – both village and castle – has its fair share of 'well-known' ghosts. Used for the exterior shots for Dr Seward's Lunatic Asylum in the movie *Dracula* (1979), the Camelot Castle Hotel is reputedly the most haunted place there. It is home to three mischievous spirits that delight in knocking paintings off walls and giving unsuspecting guests a night-time bed bath. There's also the ghost of a former employee who died during the Second World War and whose apparition has been seen along the path to the hotel from his cottage.

This poor old ghost was blamed when the cottage, previously owned by the Hollywood actress Kate Winslet, burned down in 2012 in mysterious circumstances – it was pouring with rain at the time and the cottage's electricity had been disconnected. The cause of the blaze remains a mystery.

DUCHY OR COUNTY?
1337

The Earldom of Cornwall was formed in 1068 after the Norman Conquest, helping maintain Cornwall's independence from Wessex. In 1337 Cornwall became the first Duchy – a country separate from England, not merely an English county. There are those who put these points forcefully in a desire to see Cornwall's historic independent status recognised by the UK Government. For hundreds of years the Government has refused the claim, seeing the Duchy of Cornwall as a historical quirk that has no real power in the modern world.

Cornwall's eastern boundary was fixed at the east bank of the River Tamar by Athelstan in 396 AD. The Anglo-Saxon Chronicles don't mention that Cornwall was ever conquered by the English or absorbed into the Kingdom of Wessex. Included among charters granted to Cornwall granting its right to its own parliament – Stannary charters – are the Charters of Liberties (1201, 1305 and 1402) and the Charter of Pardon (1508), which added to its rights that of veto over law passed by the Westminster government. While on paper these rights were granted in perpetuity and cannot be lawfully rescinded, they have been essentially ignored since the time of Henry VIII.

It is commonly found that during Tudor times travellers understood that the Cornish were a separate ethnic group. Lodovico Falier, an Italian diplomat at the court of Henry VIII, reported that the English, Welsh and Cornish languages were so different that they couldn't understand each other. He rather unfairly described the Cornishman as 'poor, rough and boorish'. Henry VIII even cited England and Cornwall separately in the list of his realms in his Coronation Address.

In 1535 Polydore Vergil, an Italian scholar, wrote that Britain is divided into four parts: England, Scotland, Wales and Cornwall,

all of whom 'differ emonge them selves, either in tongue, in manners, or ells in lawes and ordinaunces'. In 1616, Arthur Hopton divided England into three great provinces, England, Wales and Cornwall, '…every of them speaking a several and different language'.

Many historical maps portray Cornwall as an entity quite separate from the rest of England. Drawn by Richard of Hereford, the now-famous Mappa Mundi of 1290 (now in Hereford Cathedral) shows Cornwall depicted in its own right. On the map, Britannia Insula comprises Anglia, Cornubia, Scotia and Wallia. Indeed, many maps of Britain made prior to the 17th century show Cornwall – sometimes written as Cornubia or Cornwallia – as a nation equivalent to Wales. Sebastian Munster's simple map of 1550 shows eight of the most important areas of the British Isles, including Great Britain's main regions, namely England, Scotland, Wales and Cornwall. The maps of Flemish cartographer Abraham Ortelius (1538, 1540 and 1550) and Italian author Girolamo Ruscelli (1548) follow suit, showing a distinct country of Cornwall. Then there is a mysterious transition period, resulting in Cornwall's cartographic demotion to being an English county. I have used the word 'county' throughout this book as a general term; while accurate, the sole use of 'Duchy' may end up confusing a lot of readers!

It is certain that, with the decline of the Cornish language, outsiders began to regard Cornwall as less of an independent province, and by the 19th century the general distinction had ceased to be grasped by England and the outside world.

A PRIEST PERISHES
AT POUNDSTOCK
1357

The northern Cornish village of Poundstock appears to occupy such a tranquil location, nestled in a sleepy hollow, well out of sight of most of the world. In truth, robbery, smuggling and piracy were rife in the village from the early 14th century onwards, since it was a place where the miscreant offspring of local nobility would meet to plan their crimes in the broader country and out to sea. Even the visitation of the Black Death in 1348, which killed virtually the entire population of Poundstock, was unable to prevent the village from continuing to be used as a major centre for nefarious activities.

As twilight fell on 27 December 1357, William Penfound, clerk of the parish and survivor of the Black Death, was going about his priestly duties at mass before the altar at the parish church of St Neot in Poundstock. Suddenly, in front of the eyes of the huddled congregation, a group of men burst in and, with weapons flying, hacked the priest to death. John Grandisson, the Bishop of Exeter, placed on record what had happened:

> Certain satellites of Satan, names unknown, on the Feast of St John the Apostle – which makes the crime worse – broke into the parish church of Poundstock with a host of armed men during mass furiously entered the chancel and with swords and staves cut down William Penfound, clerk. Vestments and other church ornaments were desecrated with human blood in contempt of the Creator, in contempt of the Church. Where will we be safe from crime if the Holy Church, our Mother, the House of God and the Gateway to Heaven is thus deprived of its sanctity?

Even though a number of the men were clearly identified and actually stood trial, none of the 'Satanic satellites' were ever convicted of the murder. It all smacks of a conspiracy resulting from a local feud and vested interests, and it is likely that William Penfound, with his blood ties to the lords of the manor, was not as innocent and godly as might be imagined. In accordance with similar dramatic episodes, the murder has spawned its own ghost stories, although William Penfound's ghost is relatively benign and serene, having been seen in and about St Neot's Church going about various routine duties.

THE ANGLO-CORNISH WAR
1497

Cornwall has never been the wealthiest place in the British Isles. Times were particularly bad in the Middle Ages during the Tudor period, and a rebellion may have taken root much earlier were it not for one outstanding reason that has its roots in ancient Cornish tradition. The establishment of the Tudor dynasty, beginning with Henry VII after his defeat of Richard III at Bosworth Field in 1485, was popularly seen as a good thing by the Cornish people. The Tudors were of Welsh descent, and the fact that Arthurian tradition strongly linked Wales with Cornwall seemed to pacify the Cornish people, who generally believed that ancient prophecy was being fulfilled. Indeed, Henry VII had initially been eager to appoint loyal Cornishmen to high posts in his court. The King even named his first son Arthur and bestowed the title of Duke of Cornwall upon him.

Faced with raids and skirmishes across England's northern border by a young Yorkist pretender to the throne, Perkin Warbeck, King Henry decided to raise money for a campaign against the kingdom of Scotland. In January 1497 Parliament approved of a tax levied on 10ths or 15ths of income in all of England's shires and boroughs. Initial revenues from the new levy netted the king more than £30,000. While the king wasn't the only one in England to be smiling, there was utter fury in Cornwall. The tax had disregarded rights given to the Cornish Stannary Parliament by Edward I some 200 years before that exempted Cornwall from all taxes of 10ths or 15ths of income.

It fell to Michael An Gof, a St Keverne blacksmith, and Thomas Flamank, a Bodmin lawyer, to rouse the people of Cornwall into an armed revolt against the King. Such was the scale of discontent that it didn't take a great deal of persuasion before an army of 15,000 Cornishmen were on the march east. In Devon, the Cornish army gathered momentum as fresh provisions and recruits flowed its way. Incredibly, but for one incident at Taunton, where a tax commissioner was killed, their march was 'without any slaughter, violence or spoil of the country'. At Wells, Somerset, the noble old soldier James Touchet, 7th Baron Audley, joined the march, becoming joint political leader with Flamank. An Gof, a natural leader, remained the army's chief. Together, they issued a declaration of grievances against the Scottish War Tax.

Unopposed, they marched on to Winchester via Bristol and Salisbury. Here, it appears that there was some sort of crisis concerning how the rest of the campaign should be prosecuted. The King had remained aloof, showing an unwillingness to concede to any demands. The Cornish army realised that the matter would likely be resolved in a bloody encounter with the King's forces as they neared London. Flamank suggested that the uprising would snowball further by heading for Kent, a county that had been home to the Peasants' Revolt of 1381 and Jack Cade's rebellion against Henry VI in 1450. Yet, to the prosperous Kentish folk, Cornwall was effectively as remote as Scotland, and not only did they refuse to support the rebellion but gathered to fight the Cornish under their Earl, Edmund Grey. Dejected, the Cornish army retreated and some of the men returned home. Those remaining – about 15,000 men – were prepared to stand and do battle against the King himself.

On 13 June 1497 the Cornish army arrived at Guildford. Henry VII had recalled his army of 8,000 men, under Giles Daubeny, who had originally been intended to do battle with the Scots. The royal family and the Archbishop of Canterbury were moved to the Tower of London for safety, while panic gripped the citizens of London. Daubeney positioned his men on Hounslow Heath and were first to take the offensive. A force of 500 mounted spearmen descended on the Cornish near Guildford the following day, forcing them to move to Blackheath, from whence they had a panoramic view from the hill of the Thames and London.

On 17 June the Cornish were forced into battle against the King's army in the Battle of Deptford Bridge. Vastly inexperienced in warfare and inferior in terms of arms, the rebels were soundly defeated, up to 2,000 of them dying in the battle. After giving orders to surrender, An Gof fled but was captured in a church at Greenwich. Flamank and Touchet were both captured in the field. Touchet, a nobleman, was simply beheaded for his treason. A worse fate awaited Flamank and An Gof – on 27 June both were hung, drawn and quartered at Tyburn Hill. Flamank's last words were 'speak the truth and only then can you be free of your chains', while those of An Gof were that he should have 'a name perpetual and a fame permanent and immortal'. Their heads were hoisted on to stakes on London Bridge, their quartered bodies below making a grisly form of 'pavement art'.

Henry VII's taxes crippled Cornwall for many years to follow, forcing substantial numbers into abject poverty. On the 500th anniversary of the Cornish Rebellion a statue of Flamank and An Gof was erected in St Keverne. Presumably the blacksmith would have been delighted.

THE BATTLE OF CORNWALL

1595

On 26 July 1595, a Spanish fleet of four galleys – *Papitana, Patrona, Peregrina* and *Bazana* – under the command of Carlos de Amésquita left the Blavet Estuary in southern Brittany and set sail into the Bay of Biscay. After calling at Penmarch and sinking a ship bound for England, the Spanish vessels rounded northwestern France and crossed the Channel. On 2 August, after a voyage of 300 miles, the fleet arrived in Mount's Bay. Soon, a vicious assault on Mousehole, Paul, Newlyn and Penzance by 400 Spanish marines was under way – an attack that would today be likened to a series of surprise commando raids.

A complex historical picture involving the prolonged conflict between Catholicism and Protestantism – then raging more fiercely and fanatically than ever – forms the backdrop to the raid. Only seven years before, the Spanish Armada had been defeated. But the enmity had not ceased and, besides, this was no attempt to invade England – it was meant as a punishment, a savage kick to the underbelly of the land of Good Queen Bess. France was engaged in civil war. While the French king (known as Good King Henry) was Protestant, Philippe Emmanuel, Governor of Brittany, was a steadfast Catholic who would give any aid to a blow against England. Emmanuel accordingly helped Spain, under Philip III, continue the Anglo-Spanish War.

Since January of that year the four vessels, operating from their base in Brittany, had been venturing out on occasion to prowl the Cornish coast, harassing local shipping. They had even captured a fishing boat off St Keverne and interrogated its crew as to the aims and objectives of Francis Drake's next planned expedition. Drake and John Hawkins happened to be in Plymouth preparing for their final voyage to the West Indies. In early July, Spanish galleys had been seen at St Eval, Padstow and St Keverne.

At dawn on 2 August de Amésquita decided to take his fight to the land. After torching the town of Mousehole and Paul, he and his three companies of marines reboarded their ships. Thinking this was a prelude to an invasion, an urgent message was dispatched by Sir Francis Godolphin at Penzance to Drake in Plymouth. Meanwhile, the Spanish raiders disembarked again a couple of miles down the coast to ransack two-thirds of Penzance and burn down its fort. Newlyn was also set alight. Following their success, the Spaniards celebrated a mass on a hill near Penzance in which they promised to build a friary after England had been defeated.

By the next day, Cornish resistance had built up to such a level that the Spanish decided not to make landfall again. Were it not for a fortunate wind that struck up and enabled the galleys to make good an escape to the west, ships sent by Drake and others would have intercepted them, likely dealing them a devastating blow.

Perhaps the strangest aspect of the incident concerns an ancient Cornish prophecy that seemed to foretell the events. Sir Nicholas Clifford, one of the captains whose ship had arrived a little too late to engage the Spanish, recalled that the prophecy had been mentioned by locals, who took some comfort in it:

Ewra teyre a war meane Merlyn,
Ara Lesky Pawle Pensans ha Newlyn.

How there should land upon the rock of Merlin,
Those that would burn Paul Church, Penzance and Newlyn.

INN FOR A GOOD HAUNTING
17TH CENTURY

The Wellington Hotel in Boscastle is a fine example of a 17th-century coaching inn. Naturally enough it has its own retinue of ghostly inhabitants from ages past. While at the reception desk, Victor Tobutt, former owner of the hotel, reported seeing the figure of a man drift silently past; with his long hair tied back and wearing leather gaiters, boots, a frock coat and frilled shirt, the man appeared to have arrived straight from the 18th century. Tobutt insisted that there was nothing insubstantial about him — he looked remarkably solid until he proceeded to disappear through the wall. An employee of the hotel described having seen precisely the same thing; the apparition looked remarkably like a coachman of old.

Several members of staff, including retired policeman Bill Searle, have witnessed a less-distinct form swathed in a misty cloak drift across the landing and disappear through the wall of a guest room. For some reason the apparition is thought to be the spirit of a young woman who, having been hit hard by a disappointment in love, threw herself from the hotel's distinctive castellated tower. Another part of the hotel is reputed to be prone to the ghostly visitations of the victim of a murder. In rooms 9 and 10 the spectre of an elderly woman, caught either sitting on a bed or vanishing through the door, has been glimpsed by numerous staff and guests. One guest of July 2009 related her terrifying experience on the website Trip Advisor (corrected for clarity):

> My experience at this hotel was something I wouldn't wish upon anyone. Upon arrival and noticing it was a very old building I jokingly asked the receptionist if the hotel was haunted. She hadn't seen any ghosts but had seen a couple

of odd shadows. She did not elaborate on this and said nothing else. She then took me to my room, number 9.

We noticed a book of the hotel's history, finding a section devoted to haunting which mentioned room 9, along with a photo of outside the door of the room showing a ghostly figure. I felt very apprehensive of spending the night there. After a pleasant sleep I awoke early and decided to lie in bed and watch TV for a bit. What happened next frightened the life out of me. I suddenly felt a really strange sensation, what can only be described as someone walking up to the bed behind me, followed by a rush of cold air and then total paralysis of my body. I couldn't move for about 30 seconds, and then the feeling went as quickly as it had come. Out of fairness I think people should be informed that the hotel is haunted.

So, if you fancy a scary weekend, you know where to go ...

AWAY WITH THE FAIRIES
1645

In 1645, when she was 19 years old, Ann Jefferies entered the service of the Pitt family in St Teath, a sleepy little village between Port Isaac and Tintagel. While knitting in her employer's garden one afternoon she was startled by a rustling of the hedge, followed by the appearance of six little people with bright shining eyes, all of whom were dressed in green.

Ann claimed that the leader of the group of fairies – a little chap distinguished by a red feather in his cap – then landed on her palm. After placing him on her lap he clambered up her chest and began to kiss her neck, attention that she enjoyed so much that the other fairies soon joined in. As soon as one of the fairies ran his hands over Ann's eyes she immediately felt as though she had been pricked with a pin and she was immersed into darkness.

There followed a remarkable journey to a magical fairy realm. After speeding through the air Ann was set down, and on regaining her vision she delighted at the sight of a beautiful forested land ornamented with temples and palaces lavished with precious metals. Hundreds of normal-sized people could be seen walking about, idling, dancing and playing sport. She, too, was changed – her costume was now highly decorated, and she had no inhibitions in making love with a handsome resident of that other world. Sadly, this overt display of human-fairy affection piqued the others to such an extent that the fairy who had blinded her in the arbour had no choice but to do so again, upon which she was rapidly whisked back to reality.

But it wasn't Ann's remarkable fairy story alone that caused her fame to grow throughout England in the ensuing years. In addition to experiencing more fairy visitations it appears that her encounters had bestowed upon her a range of mystical healing powers and clairvoyance – a gift she is said to have used without asking for payment. Alarmed by Ann's growing reputation, the local authorities dispatched a group of magistrates and ministers to interview her on the nature of her otherworldly contacts. But their warnings to resist the Devil's influence and to desist in her claims and practices were not heeded, and she was soon incarcerated in Bodmin Jail. Supernatural mystery yet surrounds her three months in prison – she lived without complaint, even to the extent of refusing food from her jailers, claiming to have been sustained by nourishment delivered by the fairies.

After being freed from prison Ann lived near Padstow, where 'she liv'd a considerable time, and did many great Cures'. When interviewed just five years before she died, Ann remained adamant that her experiences were real, but she did not want her life made into 'Books or Ballads' nor her name 'spread about the country' for fear of further persecution. No, she refused to promote her astounding tale – not even for 'five hundred pounds'.

It has been suggested that Ann's altered states of consciousness may have been caused by temporal lobe seizures, well known to produce a range of weird perceptions and/or hallucinations brought about by ingesting psychotropic plants – 'magic mushrooms', for example. It appears that, in common with modern-day 'UFO abductees', she really did believe that her encounters were genuine and, like many people who claim to be in touch with aliens, she thought that psychic gifts had been bestowed upon her as a result.

A TRIPLE TRAGEDY
1648

Penfound Manor house in Poundstock, built on the site of a Saxon dwelling and around a large medieval hall, is the oldest inhabited house in England. It is thought to be the first home in the country to have had a room built specifically as a bedroom rather than a multi-function space. On 26 April 1648 Kate Penfound, daughter of prominent Civil War Royalist Arthur Penfound, decided to elope with her lover, local man John Trebarfoot. Her father would never have given his consent to the marriage, since the Trebarfoots had Parliamentarian leanings. Climbing down the manor house wall from her bedroom window she fell into her lover's arms, but just as the pair were about to make their escape they were confronted by Arthur Penfound. A terrible struggle ensued – a musket flashed, daggers were brandished – resulting in the deaths of all three.

Throughout the years there have been a number of ghost reports connected with the tragedy. Kate's ghostly face has been seen peering longingly out of the bedroom window and her spectre has been spotted drifting through the manor house. Local legend has it that on the anniversary of the tragedy all three participants can be seen re-enacting the unfortunate incident. In St Neot's Church, Poundstock, there's a memorial to John Trebarfoot with the cryptic inscription: 'That of Trebarfoot may be truly said, The love of mankind here lies buried'.

ADRIFT IN A STORM
1703

In his 1724 account of travelling from London to Land's End, Daniel Defoe describes how on 27 November 1703 a storm transported a ship, along with an unsuspecting man and two boys, from Helford to the Isle of Wight in seven hours:

The beginning of the storm there lay a ship laden with tin in Helford Haven. Between eleven and twelve o'clock the wind came about west and by south, and blew in so violent and terrible a manner that, though they rode under the lee of a high shore, yet the ship was driven from all her anchors, and about midnight drove quite out of the harbour into the open sea.

The only thing they had to think on was to keep her out at sea as far as they could, for fear of a point of land called the Dead Man's Head, which lies to the eastward of Falmouth Haven; and then, if they could escape the land, thought to run in for Plymouth next morning, so, if possible, to save their lives. In this frighted condition they drove away at a prodigious rate, having sometimes the bonnet of their foresail a little out, but the yard lowered almost to the deck – sometimes the ship almost under water, and sometimes above, keeping still in the offing, for fear of the land, till they might see daylight.

But when the day broke they found they were to think no more of Plymouth, for they were far enough beyond it; and the first land they made was Peverel Point, being the southernmost land of the Isle of Purbeck, in Dorsetshire, and a little to the westward of the Isle of Wight; so that now they were in a terrible consternation, and driving still at a prodigious rate. By seven o'clock they found themselves broadside of the Isle of Wight.

Here they consulted what to do to save their lives. One of the boys was for running her into the Downs; but the man objected that, having no anchor or cable nor boat to go on shore with, and the storm blowing off shore, they should be inevitably blown off and lost upon the unfortunate Goodwin – which, it seems, the man had been on once before and narrowly escaped.

The other of the boys said he had been in a certain creek in the Isle of Wight, where, between the rocks, he knew there was room to run the ship in. The man gave him the helm, and he stood directly in among the rocks, the people standing on the shore thinking they were mad, and that they would in a few minutes be dashed in a thousand pieces. The young bold fellow run her into a small cove, where she stuck fast, as it were, between the rocks on both sides, there being but just room enough for the breadth of the ship. The ship indeed, giving two or three knocks, staved and sunk, but the man and the two youths jumped ashore and were safe; and the lading, being tin, was afterwards secured. The merchants very well rewarded the three sailors, especially the lad that ran her into that place.

Considering that they covered a distance of some 120 miles, it must have been a terrifying experience for the Cornish sailors. Fortunately they didn't suffer the fate of Defoe's most famous creation, Robinson Crusoe, or they would have been stranded on the Isle of Wight for 28 years!

DISASTER AT SEA
1707

Flushed with naval warfare success in the Mediterranean during the summer of 1707, Sir Cloudesley Shovell, commander-in-chief of the British fleets, was ordered to bring his fleet back to England. The fleet contained an impressive 21 vessels, of which 15 were ships of the line – HMS *Association* (Shovell's own flagship), *Royal Anne, Torbay, St George, Cruizer, Eagle, Lenox, Monmouth, Orford, Panther, Romney, Rye, Somerset, Swiftsure* and *Valeur* – along with fireships HMS *Firebrand, Griffin, Phoenix* and *Vulcan*, the sloop *Weazel* and the yacht *Isabella*.

Setting out from Gibraltar on 29 September, the passage north was beset by worsening storms and high winds, pushing them off their planned course. Astronomical observations ordered by Shovell to determine the fleet's latitude – what would normally have been a relatively easy task, compared with finding longitude – were made extremely difficult, given the poor conditions. On the night of 22 October the fleet entered the English Channel. After consulting his navigational officers, Shovell thought that they were probably at a safe distance west of the island of Ushant near the northwestern tip of Brittany. One officer disagreed – the master of *Lenox* reckoned that they were to the west of the Isles of Scilly, much further north.

Rather than ride out the night by ordering the fleet west to certain safety, the 21 ships continued on their course. Before long they had hit the rocks west of the Scilly Isles. HMS *Association* struck the Outer Gilstone Rock at 8 p.m and sank within a few minutes. Its entire crew of 800 were lost, including Shovell. Following it, *St George* and *Phoenix* also hit the rocks, but stayed afloat. HMS *Firebrand* was not so fortunate, hitting the same rocks and later sinking with the loss of two-thirds of its crew. HMS *Eagle* collided with the Crim Rocks and sank shortly afterwards near Bishop Rock, all crew being lost. HMS *Romney* hit Bishop Rock itself, sinking with just a sole survivor. It is still not known how many officers, sailors and marines perished on that fateful night, but estimates range from between 1,400 to more than 2,000. It was one of the worst maritime disasters in British naval history, and a low point for the Royal Navy.

Shovell's body was washed up at Porthellick Cove on St Mary's the following day, seven miles from his wrecked ship. His shirt was missing and his left finger was minus a precious emerald ring. One story alleges that the Admiral was alive when he clawed his way ashore, but was murdered by a woman for the sake of the ring (the Isles of Scilly had a piratical reputation as bad as mainland Cornwall at the time). Another myth emerged on Scilly that a common Jack Tar on HMS *Association* had been hanged at the yardarm by Shovell for warning that the fleet was off course; it was claimed that grass will never grow at Shovell's first burial place at Porthellick Cove because the sailor who was so cruelly punished for giving the warning was a Scillonian.

A board of enquiry determined that the disaster's chief cause was a navigational inability to calculate longitude accurately. This led to the Longitude Act of 1714, the establishment of the Board of Longitude and the Navy's quest for an accurate marine chronometer. The wrecks were rediscovered 260 years later, and in 1970 at an auction of some items recovered by divers, the sum of £270 was fetched for Shovell's chamber pot.

SUPERNATURAL SMUGGLER
1713

Cornwall's remoteness from the rest of the UK and its close relationship with the sea, made ever-more intimate by its shoreline packed with coves, harbours, bays and estuaries, has given rise to centuries of smuggling enterprises. Some small, some big, some modest and some audacious in their scope, schemes of smuggling once formed an integral part of the Cornish economy. 'The coasts here swarm with smugglers from the Land's End to the Lizard,' wrote George Borlase in 1753. He wasn't exaggerating in the slightest.

Increasing involvement by revenue agents in the 18th century, along with more severe penalties for those caught involved in smuggling, threatened not only a long-established way of life but caused genuine hardship among the local population. Although a scourge to the law of the land, smugglers were popularly considered bold, brave, even heroic – and some of them undoubtedly were.

Talland, on the southeast coast of Cornwall, was the setting for one of the most unusual ways in which smuggling activities were disguised. Legend has it that Talland parish church, atop the cliffs overlooking Looe Bay, was built at its present site because each time work commenced at the intended location its stones would somehow be transported overnight to its current cliff-top setting. The superstitious masons quickly heeded the supernatural sign and proceeded to build the church where the unknown stone-shifters had suggested. It now seems probable that smugglers needed the church to be placed on a cliff-top location in order for signals to be communicated to and from contraband-laden vessels at sea.

Richard Dodge, vicar of Talland between 1713 and 1747, gained quite a reputation as a ghost hunter and exorcist. He claimed the divine power to be able to cast away evil spirits and drive away the Devil; indeed, he even told the story of having seen the Devil straining at the reins of a sable coach drawn by two headless horses. According to Dodge, Bridle Lane – a path that led from the village to the beach – was infested with all manner of demonic entities. His warnings were heeded by the parishioners, and few God-fearing people ever ventured down there at night. This conveniently enabled smugglers – of whose illegal fraternity Dodge himself was a leading member – to use Bridle Lane without much fear of being caught.

Smuggling carried on long after Dodge. Inside the church can be found the headstone of Robert Mark, thought to have been a Polperro smuggler shot at sea by a customs officer in 1802. It reads:

> In prime of life, most suddenly, Sad tidings to relate,
> Here view my utter destiny, And pity my sad state.
> I by a shot which rapid flew, Was instantly struck dead.
> Lord pardon the offender who My precious blood did shed.

Nice to know there were no hard feelings ...

SITTING COMFORTABLY
1713

These days we're used to reading about celebrities and eccentrics whose last wish was to be buried with a selection of their most loved possessions, in their rock-and-roll regalia or inside their favourite car. Such requests were most unusual in the past, where respect for religious solemnity tended to override an individual's personal desires. James Tillie (1645–1713) was a notable exception. He was buried in style.

Born to a poor family, Tillie rose through the ranks working for Sir John Coryton, wealthy owner of the Newton Ferrers estate near Saltash. After Sir John's death in mysterious circumstances in 1680, Tillie married his widow Elizabeth, and commissioned the building of Pentillie, a large country house on the estate. Tillie ordered that on his death he should be buried in a specially built mausoleum on the estate's 'Mount Ararat'. It was not to be a run-of-the-mill interment. He insisted that his body be clothed in its finest garments and laid to rest sitting upright, bound to his favourite chair, with smoking pipe and books to hand and facing out of a window overlooking the estate. Thinking that the Day of Judgment was imminent, Tillie ordered that his servants were to carry on bringing him food and wine, so that he was thoroughly prepared for the resurrection.

On Tillie's death in 1713 his orders were duly carried out. But after two years his servants, realising that the resurrection might be a way off yet, decided to abandon the daily meal deliveries. Pentillie was extensively remodelled during the early 19th century, and Tillie's body was thought to have been removed from his *vista mortis* and reburied. No records were made of the site of the re-interment, but later historians assumed that a nearby churchyard was used.

In 2013 archaeologists working on the site of the old mausoleum at Pentillie made an exciting discovery – inside a brick vault they found Tillie's remains, exactly 300 years after he had originally been placed there, surrounded by what was left of his earthly paraphernalia. Pentillie's owner, Ted Coryton, said there was no doubt that the remains belonged to Tillie. He was toasted with sloe gin and the vault was closed up once more.

CLAY COUNTRY
1745

There are a few places or areas in the United Kingdom whose identities – right down to their very names – are based on the industry that takes (or took) place there. Many of these, such as the Black Country (western West Midlands), Steel City (Sheffield) and the Potteries (the six towns of Stoke-on-Trent), received their well-known appellations in the Industrial Revolution. Yet few people think of Cornwall as having been affected by that great era of burgeoning industry and new technology. The fact is, Cornwall has been just as much altered and scarred by industrial progress as any other 18th-century region that harboured resources to plunder. It's just that the landscape in question – the Clay Country – is, for the most part, conveniently located out of sight of anyone but the locals, and well off the tracks most often followed by tourists.

We get a prolonged but distant glimpse of Clay Country as we travel down the A30, beyond the town of Bodmin. Looming above the horizon on the other side of the road can be seen substantial uplands, interspersed with curious geometrical mounds, some of them bright and gleaming like freshly pointed pyramids. These are the strange pyramids of Clay Country – giant masses of debris, some of them hundreds of feet high, piled up by many decades of relentless mining of precious china clay. These formations appear as out of place in this naturally undulating landscape as would a volcano in Kent. Sometimes known as the Cornish Alps, their slopes and saddles are hugged by villages that for centuries have been in their thrall. The china clay industry is still a major employer in Cornwall, especially within Clay Country itself where the majority of working adults are reliant on it.

Cornwall's china clay industry began in 1745 when William Cookworthy – a chemist from Plymouth – found a natural material that could be used in the manufacture of porcelain. Until then, porcelain was manufactured solely in China and was very expensive to import. Kaolin, the material that he discovered at Tregonning Hill near Germoe, was a form of decomposed granite that could be processed using water and made into a usable clay with remarkable translucent qualities when fired. Cookworthy developed the process and within a few decades it became big business.

Most of the deposits were to be found below the surface of the desolate but beautiful moorland heights of central Cornwall. Over the course of 250 years this unique landscape has been dug out relentlessly, ravaged by the quest for kaolin; it is beautiful in places, but mainly it's an artificial beauty. Parts of Clay Country resemble the moon, with vast open terraced pits, some of whose depths are filled with water that takes on a stunning aquamarine, emerald or turquoise hue. Indeed, the bright spots of exposed rock in Clay Country amalgamate into a single patch of brilliance that can clearly be seen from the moon itself.

A FLASH MOB,
FLUSHED
1745

Methodist preacher John Wesley (1703–91) travelled extensively throughout Cornwall as he conveyed to those who would listen his own 'no-frills' brand of Christianity. His journals give the reader an insight into not only the founder of Methodism but the nature and attitudes of the Cornish of two and a half centuries ago. Wesley's preachments eventually took root in Cornwall, but he was by no means universally liked in the county, nor was his message particularly welcomed by all.

Wesley's journal entry of 4 July 1745 relates a remarkable episode in which, while visiting a gentlewoman in Falmouth, an angry, baying crowd of hundreds of people surrounded the house, demanding that they should deal with Wesley. 'The house was beset on all sides by an innumerable multitude of people,' he wrote, 'a louder or more confused noise could hardly be at the taking of a city by storm. The rabble roared with all their throats.'

The fuming crowd were joined by a group of hardened privateers who had just come ashore. Eager to join in the fun, they thrust their way forward and smashed down the door, shouting, 'Avast, lads, avast!' (this might seem an unlikely cry, even given that they were mariners, considering that its actual meaning is 'Stop' or 'Cease' – but the words appear in Wesley's journal). And then something quite remarkable happened. Taking off his hat, and speaking so low as to be scarcely audible to the mob, Wesley identified himself and simply asked why he was wanted. The crowd went silent. No more curses were uttered, no more objects thrown at the preacher, and the privateers didn't even steal his purse. He was allowed to go on his way, unmolested.

Wesley himself considered this to be a near-miraculous episode. Indeed, the end result was in contrast to the way in which the itinerant preacher was treated around the country (including other places in Cornwall). He compares it with his recent rough handling by a mob in Walsall, where he had been dragged by his hair from the podium, carried through the streets by a group demanding he be killed, and assaulted before he made an escape into the countryside.

CORNISH TSUNAMI
1755

On the morning of 1 November 1755 a megathrust earthquake well exceeding magnitude 8.7 ripped through the oceanic crust 150 miles off the southwestern corner of Portugal. It was one of the largest earthquakes in history, and at 9.40 a.m. the Portuguese city of Lisbon fell victim to the event. The old city, a major cultural centre of Europe, so full of architectural wonder, was virtually demolished in one stroke. What hadn't initially been destroyed was later swept away by the ensuing tsunami, burned down or shaken to the ground in one of many violent aftershocks in the weeks that followed. Tens of thousands of people were killed in the Lisbon area alone, and according to some estimates, up to a hundred thousand folk were killed in the wider region.

Propagating away from the earthquake's epicentre, the tsunami hit the Cornish coast, over 1,000 miles away, at around 2 p.m. Reports counted three main waves. At St Michael's Mount, the sea rapidly rose six feet, ebbed just as fast, and then continued to yo-yo, rising and falling in a diminishing cycle for around five hours. Geologist William Borlase wrote: 'The sea was observed at the Mount-pier to advance suddenly from the eastward.' Another witness stated that 'the sea advanced with such impetuosity that large round blocks of granite were swept along like pebbles'. One person is said to have been killed. At Penzance the sea rose by a maximum of eight feet, but was highest at Newlyn, where it reached ten feet.

There's no official record of the general death toll, but the 19th-century French seismologist Arnold Boscowitz claimed that 'great loss of life and property occurred upon the coasts of Cornwall'. The tsunami continued up the English Channel, affecting coastal areas further east to a lesser extent, and it even caused the Thames in London to rise by several feet.

Ironically, just 17 days later, at 4.30 a.m. on 18 November, another major earthquake had an impact on Cornwall – that is, the towns of Cornwall, Connecticut, and Cornwall, Pennsylvania – which were shaken by the Cape Ann earthquake off the Massachusetts coast.

A GEORGIAN EARTHQUAKE
1757

One of the largest earthquakes to hit Cornwall took place on the beautiful summer's evening of 15 July 1757 at 6.30 p.m. The earthquake – whose epicentre was in the Penzance area – is estimated to have been around magnitude 4.4 on the Richter Scale, quite a substantial earth-shaker that produced large effects across Cornwall and the Scilly Isles, and it was detected further afield in Devon. Since the modern sensitive seismometer wasn't put into general scientific use until the late 19th century, we have only the written testimony of those who experienced the earthquake by which to judge its size and scale.

The earthquake was to prompt an account by William Borlase in the *Philosophical Transactions of the Royal Society* of 1759. Based on 19 detailed records from 18 locations, the account was the first detailed scientific study of a British earthquake. Tin miners deep beneath the ground at St Just, Lannant and Godolphin feared for their lives as rock was shaken loose from the tunnel walls and roofs. Miners at Gwinear and Chacewater seem only to have been alarmed by a noise 'as if the loose rubbish of the mines was set in motion'.

Founder of the Methodist movement John Wesley happened to be spreading his particular brand of the Word in Cornwall at the time. According to Wesley's journal, 'there was first a rumbling noise under the ground, hoarser and deeper than common thunder. Then followed a trembling of the earth, which afterwards waved once or twice to and fro.' So violently did the ground move that people reported being scarcely able to remain standing as the walls around them seemed to be on the point of collapse.

One unfortunate chap who happened to be in precisely the wrong place at the wrong time proved to be the only fatality of the 1757 earthquake. Seated at an upstairs window in his home in Penryn,

Stephen Thomas was alarmed so much that he fell backwards, tumbled to the ground and sustained fatal injuries.

I can imagine exactly what the Penzance earthquake felt like, having experienced the Dudley earthquake during the small hours of 22 September 2002, which was of a similar magnitude. A loud rumbling noise was certainly one of the most notable features, along with the nauseating feeling that the ground was about to give way. As for larger earthquakes – I cannot imagine how terrifying those must be.

Incredibly, substantial earthquakes hit Norwich, Yorkshire and Wales in the same year, but none were as strong as the Cornish quake. Like other parts of the UK, Cornwall is prone to its own 'home-grown' earthquakes. There are two main areas prone to seismic activity beneath Cornwall – one in the northeast and another in the southwest, with a small centre between the two beneath St Austell.

In 1775, just days after a large earthquake in Swansea, St Austell was shaken, several stacks of chimneys tumbled to the ground and a stable at a coaching inn collapsed. Seven major rumbles have occurred in Cornwall since then: 1783 (Launceston), 1852 (Callington), 1858 (Liskeard), 1859 (Padstow), 1860 (Newquay) and 1883 (Launceston); there were no large Cornish quakes in the 20th century, the latest having taken place on 4 December 2011 (in Bodmin), a magnitude 2.2 event that I felt while seated in the very chair from which I'm writing.

Finally, it's worth mentioning that in a paper published in the *Proceedings of the Royal Society of Cornwall* of 1845, a study of earthquakes showed them to occur at times when the moon was closest to the Earth. On checking the data, it seems that the moon was near its furthest point *from* Earth on the date of the 1757 quake, but it was very close to new moon, a time when the combined gravitational pull of sun and moon are near maximum. The next two sets of lunar circumstances close to the 1757 quake (with the moon in about the same place in the sky) take place on 14/15 July 2015 and 2034. You have been warned!

THE DEVIL'S FOOTPRINTS
1757

If you're a keen follower of paranormal tales from bygone ages you may be curious as to why the mystery of the 'Devil's Footprints' is recounted here. In case you're not familiar with the story, it concerns the appearance on the morning of 9 February 1855 of curious hoof-shaped tracks in a fresh fall of snow that ran in straight lines over all manner of obstacles – fences, trees, walls, roofs – across a hundred miles of south Devon. This is the more famous case of the Devil's Footprints, and while close to Cornwall, it doesn't count! No, our mysterious diabolical imprints were created a little more than a century before in the warm summer sands of Penzance.

As soon as people had recovered their equilibrium after the Penzance earthquake of 15 July 1757, they were astonished to find a 100-square-yard area of the beach covered with thousands of marks like circular hoof prints. The marks were described as 'little cones surrounded by basins of equal diameter' and as having 'black specks on the tops of cones, as if something, perhaps gaseous, had issued from them'. One of these curious formations was observed to issue 'a gush of water as thick as a man's wrist' like a mini-geyser.

Some of the more superstitious locals began thinking that the marks were caused in a taunting celebratory dance given by the Devil, for they appeared in plain view of St Michael's Mount, a place that had been built in honour of his greatest adversary, the Archangel St Michael.

This phenomenon, long held to be a prime example of a 'Fortean' phenomenon (after Charles Fort, a prolific collector of strange tales during the early 20th century) seems to have a mundane explanation, a fact admitted by Fort himself. Shifting ground has long been known to cause liquefaction during earthquakes, where waterlogged ground can be shaken loose to produce localised flooding; it can be forced through fissures in mud to form little mud 'volcanoes'. But the very specific location of these strange features and the odd black dots cannot easily be explained, and they have never been reported since in Cornwall.

Another example of the Devil's Footprints in Cornwall can be found near St Peter's Church in Newlyn, atop a striking outcrop of rocks known as the Tolcarne. The place is thought to have been used as a sacred site in pagan times (it may still serve as a venerated centre of strange practices) and is known locally as the Devil's Rock. Carved into the solid granite at the Tolcarne's summit are some curious markings that local legend claims to be the footprints of the Devil. The story goes that the Devil was caught stealing nets from the local fishermen, and while being pursued tripped and left his footprints in the solid rock. Turning angrily on his pursuers he raised himself upright, and spreading wide his monstrous bat-wings cried, 'Bucca! Bucca! Bucca!' (*see also* p78–9) as fire spurted from his mouth.

WESLEY'S TORNADO
1760

John Wesley's 18th-century journals are not exclusively devoted to spiritual and ecclesiastical affairs. They are a fascinating account of one man's travels, and Cornwall features prominently in them. One of the more interesting meteorological phenomena recounted by Wesley concerns 'a kind of waterspout' that was seen on 27 May 1760:

> Wednesday, 17 [June 1760]. The room at St. Just was quite full at five, and God gave us a parting blessing. At noon I preached on the cliff near Penzance, where no one now gives an uncivil word. Here I procured an account, from an eyewitness, of what happened the twenty-seventh of last month. A round pillar, narrowest at bottom, of a whitish color, rose out of the sea near Mousehole and reached the clouds. One who was riding over the strand from Marazion to Penzance saw it stand for a short space and then move swiftly toward her, till the skirt of it touching her, the horse threw her and ran away. It had a strong sulphurous smell. It dragged with it abundance of sand and pebbles from the shore; and then went over the land, carrying with it corn, furze, or whatever it found in its way. It was doubtless a kind of waterspout; but a waterspout on land, I believe, is seldom seen.

Wesley was obviously impressed by this phenomena, because two days later he returned to the subject, noting that it had picked up 'eighteeen stacks of corn, with a large haystack', and 'scattered them abroad'.

A ROTTEN MP
1784

At 120 feet high, the perpendicular 'Somerset'-style tower of the church of St Probus is the tallest of any in the county and can be seen for miles around. Beneath that tower, so imposing an accomplishment, spreads a fascinating old graveyard, and one impressive tomb fascinates more than any of the others. Standing proud above ground and guarded at its four corners by elaborately sculpted soldiers in royalist uniform, the chest tomb is inscribed to the memory of Sir Christopher Hawkins (1758–1829). This splendid monument would suggest a man of high repute and honour – but nothing could be further from the truth.

Ever since his older brother John had drowned in the Thames while at Eton and his younger brother Thomas had died of a 'fever in consequence of eating an ice-cream after dancing', Christopher Hawkins had developed what might be called a neurotic paranoid personality. Taking on the mantle of family head, and following in his wealthy father's footsteps, he became MP for Grampound and various other Cornish boroughs between 1784 and his death.

Parliament hasn't always been as accountable as it is today, and you don't have to dig very far into history to see that corruption and blatant unfairness was endemic in the way that the ruling classes governed the country. One of the most striking examples of this can be found in the unreformed House of Commons (Parliament as it existed prior to the Reform Act of 1832) and the rotten boroughs of Cornwall. Before 1832, constituencies were arranged in a haphazard manner, with little bearing on their size or population. Cornwall was hugely over-represented in Parliament. Some boroughs had such tiny populations that the bribery or coercion of a relative few could 'buy' the seat – these were known as 'rotten boroughs'.

To this end, Hawkins consolidated his power and bought more than a dozen manors across the county; it was said that Cornwall could not be crossed from north to south without stepping on anything but Hawkins' soil. With such property, influence and power, Hawkins had ownership or part-ownership of six such Cornish boroughs and was able to ensure the successful election of candidates (usually Tory government supporters) in return for money or favours. After being made a baronet in 1791 by William Pitt the Younger, Hawkins continued in his old ways, unrepentant and blatantly corrupt.

Following the 1806 Penryn election, a parliamentary committee accused Hawkins of 'boroughmongering' and bribery, causing him to be ousted from his seat. His trial at Bodmin Assizes turned into a sham, and following his acquittal Hawkins declared a pistol duel with his main accuser. Nobody was injured and the pretence of honour was satisfied. Despite growing common knowledge of corruption, the system was so biased and immune to opinion that Hawkins managed to get himself re-elected several times for Penryn and St Ives.

By all accounts, Christopher Hawkins had a deeply unimpressive personality. He spoke in Parliament just four times, always briefly and in an incoherent, inaudible mumble. He was so miserly that he deprived people of their homes on his land to reduce election expenses; it got to the stage where his borough of Mitchell contained just three people eligible to vote. A sign was said to have once been fixed to the gates of his estate at Trewithen:

A large house, and no cheer,
A large park, and no deer,
A large cellar, and no beer,
Sir Christopher Hawkins lives here.

He died in 1829 after receiving a vaccination for smallpox – ironically, a disease that had been a lifelong fear of his.

THE PELTING POLTERGEIST
1821

Carlow Street in Truro was, to all appearances, an ordinary residential place. In April 1821 it appeared that somebody in the area was playing tricks by throwing sizeable stones from a distance towards one particular house in the street – an activity that threatened to do some serious damage to person or property if kept up. Despite the best efforts of the residents of the house, and then other residents of Carlow Street, the perpetrator remained elusive. In those days throwing a stone could land you in serious trouble – even transportation to Australia if it caused a window to shatter or took someone's eye out.

The stones kept on landing, here and there around the house, from one day to the next and at all hours. Some inhabitants, thinking that a practical joke was in progress, were amused. Others were alarmed, believing that the peace of the community was being disrupted by some unseen malignant will, be the stones thrown by a living person's hand or – possibly – cast under the direction of some malicious supernatural entity.

Soon after the story began to propagate, the Mayor of Truro, John Bennallak, decided to go along to Carlow Street to see for himself. Initially confident that the whole affair was either mischief or a hoax, it appears that he ended up being made so nervous by the rattling stones that he called out a military guard. While investigating the situation along with the soldiers, the stones continued to pepper the property. The stone-throwing continued into May, but the frequency gradually diminished. No cause for the incident – which has a number of parallels in other places over the centuries, including modern times – was ever identified.

MOVERS AND SHAKERS
1824

What happens when an irresistible force encounters a very moveable object? The irresistible force in question was His Majesty's Navy, in the form of an intoxicated Lieutenant Hugh Goldsmith and a dozen similarly inebriated sailors from HMS *Nimble*. The moveable object: Logan Rock, an 80-ton granite boulder perched atop the cliffs of a small peninsula near the village of Treen, Land's End.

Known as *Men Omborth* in Cornish (meaning 'balanced stone'), Logan Rock is perhaps the most famous British example of a very large, naturally balanced stone that responds by rocking to the touch yet is so massive that it refuses to budge further, regardless of the individual's most strenuous efforts. Countless millennia of weathering through natural fissures in the rock creates these amazing petrological phenomena, and it's not surprising that they often crop up in folklore and legend. Logan Rock was featured in the lyric drama *Caractacus* (1759) by William Mason:

> Turn your astonish'd eyes; behold yon huge
> And unhewn sphere of living adamant,
> Which, poised by magic, rests its central weight
> On yonder pointed rock: firm as it seems,
> Such is the strange and virtuous property,
> It moves obsequious to the gentlest touch
> Of him whose breast is pure.

In April 1824, Lt Goldsmith rowed ashore with his men and clambered up the cliffs to Logan Rock. In the full knowledge of the rock's great renown – adulation, even, by many locals – the sailors were enthusiastically given the task of dislodging it. Crowbars, levers and brute strength soon did the trick, and after tumbling down the headland Logan Rock became firmly wedged in a crevice.

It's interesting to note that the lieutenant was a nephew of writer and poet Oliver Goldsmith; perhaps he had read too much into the title of his famous uncle's work, *An History of the Earth and Animated Nature*, which had been published just two years before. Surely the dislodging of Logan Rock was a supreme example of animated nature!

In what was an act of cultural vandalism the like of which had not been seen since Henry VIII's dissolution of the monasteries in the mid-16th century, Lt Goldsmith's wanton dethronement of Logan Rock from its age-old position overlooking the Atlantic shocked Cornwall and appalled the rest of the country. Thousands of complaints were conveyed to the Admiralty, and consequently Goldsmith was ordered to replace the rock in its original position at his own expense. Thankfully Logan Rock had not smashed to smithereens, and apart from minor chips and scratches appeared relatively unscathed by its fall. By November, a team of 60 labourers using equipment loaned by the Admiralty managed to hoist the rock into its original place, much to the delight of thousands of spectators. Sadly, the original finger-touch sensitivity of Logan Rock was impossible to restore: a hefty shove to induce it to rock was the best they could do. In total, the procedure cost Goldsmith £105 and the Admiralty £25 – not far short of £10,000 in today's money. The wall of The Logan Rock pub in Treen displays the original invoice for equipment and labour, and the anchor holes for the hoisting tackle remain visible in the surrounding cliff.

A CORNISH WAVE IN MEXICO
1825

Real del Monte, a small town in southeastern Mexico's Hidalgo state, is rather atypical of that country's municipalities. At first glance there's nothing particularly striking about the landscape or the architecture of the place – a mass of low-level houses with white walls and red-tiled roofs intermingled with the deep lush greenery of palm, poinsettia, jacaranda and mango trees. But look to the hills beyond and you'll see, rising from the vegetation, a number of dark structures that appear strangely out of place. Closer inspection will reveal that these towers house the lifting machinery for deep mines hewn into the district's hard volcanic rock in order to access silver-rich veins. Much of the old mining infrastructure came from more than 5,000 miles away and was set up by settlers of a distinctly un-Latino nature – Cornishmen who brought the Industrial Revolution and prosperity to this sleepy, subtropical part of the world, and stayed for generations to establish their own bit of Cornwall in Mexico.

Look again at the roofs of the houses of Real del Monte – unique to Mexico, many of them are pitched, an innovation brought by the Cornish settlers.

Years of Civil War and the struggle for Mexico's independence from Spain in the early 19th century had ruined Mexico's once-prosperous but basic mining industry. By complete contrast, the Cornish mining industry was booming, at the forefront of world mining technology. In an attempt to restart the economy, the new independent Mexica government sold the land, known to be silver-rich, to the British-backed Real del Monte Mining Company.

In 1825 a band of 60 Cornishmen left Falmouth and Camborne and set sail for Mexico, taking with them with 1,500 tons of the latest heavy-duty mining machinery. Their initial reception on reaching those far western shores was chilly – the Spanish-held port of Veracruz turned them away, and the mining mission was forced to debark on a beach at Mocambo. From here, with the hired help of hundreds of locals, they lugged their machinery through hostile, mosquito-infested jungle and swamp to Santa Fe. The trek took a heavy toll on the expedition – malaria and yellow fever resulted in the deaths of half the Cornish and a hundred Mexicans, and the rainy season was upon them. After temporarily abandoning their equipment to escape into the mountains to Xalapa, three months later they resumed their journey. On 1 May 1826, after an arduous 250-mile trek in which their heavy machinery had been carried to an altitude of 10,000 feet above sea level, the group finally arrived at Real del Monte.

Despite its hazardous beginnings, the miners' mission proved extremely successful. The Cornish community soon flourished as precious ores were hewn from the rock, bringing wealth and employment, not only to the town but to the miners' families back home. The miners introduced remittances as a form of payment, which helped build the Wesleyan Chapel in Redruth in the 1820s. Among the Cornish influences on local culture was the introduction of the Cornish pasty, Methodism, traditional Cornish hymn singing and Cornish wrestling. Mexico's first football club, Pachuca Athletic, was originally made up entirely of Cornishmen – they even won the first championship tournament of the Mexican Football League in 1907.

The Mexican Revolution of 1910, led by Villa and Zapata, put paid to the chances of the continuing presence of foreign enterprise in Mexico, and most of the Cornish miners of Real del Monte, and some of the descendants of the original group, made their way back to Cornwall. Today, their legacy lives on in many ways. Four Cornish engine houses remain, and so does a cemetery containing the graves of hundreds of Cornish people who operated the engines when they were working. The town has Cornish Mining Museums and a Cornish-Mexican Cultural Society, and while the pasty remains a food relished by the locals it's virtually unheard of in the rest of Mexico. The first International Cornish Pasty Festival was held there in 2009, and in the same year the town was twinned with Redruth.

A GRUESOME GRAPPLE
1826

Accounts of a special style of wrestling in Cornwall date back to the 15th Century – a banner showing grappling Cornish wrestlers flew in the breeze at Agincourt – and it is likely that the sport goes back more than a thousand years. Contenders from Cornwall, Devon and Brittany have wrestled in inter-Celtic bouts since 1402 – the latest such event, held in 2006 at Wadebridge, saw the Heavyweight Champion of Cornwall, Ashley Cawley, defeat his Breton opponent to take the crown.

Of the different styles of Celtic wresting, Cornish wrestling is the most 'gentlemanly'. Contenders wear strong jackets to provide a grip on their opponent, and the objective is to throw the opponent onto his back as flat as possible. Devon wrestling, which was at its most popular in the nineteenth Century, was far harder – it allowed contenders to wear toughened shoes so that the opponent could be kicked as well as grappled.

What was to be history's greatest West Country wrestling match took place on the Cornwall-Devon border at Tamar Green, Morice Town (now part of Plymouth) on 23 October 1826. Squaring up to each other in front of a crowd of more than 12,000, were 'big' James Polkinghorne of St Columb Major, Cornwall, and 'nimble' Abraham Cann of Colebrooke, Devon. At stake was a prize of £200 – equivalent to £20,000 in today's money. The pairing couldn't have seemed less even. 38-year-old Polkinghorne was a Champion Cornish wrester, 6ft 2in tall and weighing 22 stone; having been a pub landlord for a number of years he was not in top form. 32-year-old Abraham Cann, Champion Devon wrestler, was just 5ft 8in tall and weighed 12½ stone. Cann had two big advantages over the Cornish giant – he was fresh, having defeated James Warren of Redruth the previous month – and he was wearing shoes whose points were as hard as flint. The grip of neither wrestler had ever been overcome once their opponent had been clinched.

The rivals' efforts were superb. Cann depended on his agility to save him, but Polkinghorne soon gathered his head under his arm, and lifting him from the ground, threw him clean over his shoulder and planted him on his back; the very earth groaned with the uproar that followed. Bets were halted when it appeared that the Cornishman was headed for victory. But the second round went to the Devon man; despite falling into his opponent's grip, he managed to smash his rock-solid boot into his off-balanced opponent's leg and threw him to the ground. Round four saw two breathless wrestlers playing for time; Cann was first to recover, but maintaining a pretence of fatigue, quickly ducked beneath Polkinghorne and threw him to his back. By round eight Polkinghorne was on his last legs – and what legs they were, bruised and gashed all over by Cann's hefty boots. Shoeless, Polkinghorne maintained his Cornish wrestling style throughout, never lashing out at his opponent at any point.

Disputes among the umpires delayed the onset of the tenth round by an hour. Competing with absolute fury, and taking Cann's bone-splintering kicks with contempt, Polkinghorne gripped his opponent with the strength of a bear, lifted him in his arms, turned him head-over-heels and dashed him to the ground with stunning force. Thinking that victory was his, the Cornishman dropped to his knees.

But the fall was disputed, and the turn was disallowed. Amid a mighty clamour, Polkinghorne stormed out of the ring. Claiming default, Cann was declared the winner, and he walked off with the prize money, covered with blood and contusions.

Attempts were made to get the pair together for a rematch, but Polkinghorne refused to meet Cann unless he discarded his shoes. Each wrestler continued to live with a wholesome dread of the other. Polkinghorne – the rightful victor – continued to manage the Red Lion at St Columb Major, where he died in 1854. Cann retired to Colebrooke, also becoming a pub landlord. In 1861, three years before he died, Lord Palmerston presented him with £200 that had been raised in his honour.

THE ECCENTRIC VICAR
OF MORTENSTOW
1835

Atop Higher Sharpnose Point, a cliff around half a mile west of the village of Mortenstow in northeast Cornwall, can be admired two of the National Trust's most remarkable properties – Lundy, one of its largest, and Hawker's Hut, its very smallest.

Lundy, measuring three miles by a mile and a half, is the largest island off the southwest coast and lies 22 miles north from this point on the coast. It takes its name from the old Norse for 'puffin island' and in addition to being a National Trust property it is a renowned Site of Special Scientific Interest. Although geographically closer to Devon than Cornwall and with more recent historical ties, Lundy has ancient links with Cornwall that date back to the Neolithic period, evident in ancient sites that bear a strong resemblance to those found in Cornwall.

This fact was well known and appreciated by Reverend Robert Hawker (1803–75), the builder of Hawker's Hut, a ramshackle wooden booth as large as a garden shed, set into the hillside and roofed with turf to shield it from the extremities of the weather. It has stood there for more than 150 years. From his unusual cliff-top perch, Hawker spent endless hours away from his vicarage and church in nearby Mortenstow, contemplating on a good many things, from Arthurian legend to smugglers, while puffing away at an opium-laden pipe. Alfred Tennyson and Charles Kingsley were just two of the illustrious guests to spend time with him in his hut.

There had been no vicar at the church of St Morwenna and St John the Baptist at Mortenstow for more than a century when Hawker took the job in 1835. After honeymooning with his first wife Charlotte at Tintagel, Hawker relished the chance of invigorating the local spirit.

In addition to renovating the ancient church and building a vicarage whose chimneys were shaped like the towers of significant churches in his life, in 1843 he single-handedly invented the modern custom of the Harvest Festival.

Hawker extended his compassion beyond the cliffs and was often first on the scene to organise the rescue of shipwrecked crews; monuments to the ships *Caledonia* and *Alonzo*, wrecked in 1842 and 1843 respectively, can be seen in the churchyard, where those who lost their lives were buried.

As you might have gathered by now, Hawker was by no means conventional. Little of the clergyman's black attire appealed to him, except the socks. Loving bright colours, he often wore a claret coat, blue jumper, thigh-high sea boots, a pink cap and a yellow poncho (claiming that it was the garment King Arthur had tried to steal from St Padarn in the 6th century). He enthusiastically welcomed all visitors to his church, including his own nine cats, one of whom was foolish enough to catch a mouse on a Sunday; its penalty was excommunication.

A keen poet, in his younger days Hawker wrote 'The Song of the Western Men', better known as 'Trelawny' and now the unofficial Cornish national anthem. Unpredictable to the end, this Anglican vicar converted to Catholicism on his deathbed.

THE EGYPTIAN HOUSE
1835

The streets of central Penzance are full of architectural delights spanning many hundreds of years, but none are so utterly unexpected and flamboyantly delightful as one particular building on Chapel Street. Known as the Egyptian House, this fabulously colourful and ornate Grade I listed building is sandwiched between two smaller, far plainer Georgian buildings. Those who come upon this remarkable edifice by chance might well rub their eyes to make sure they're not seeing things.

Following Napoleon's Egyptian campaigns and the work of the Egyptologist Champollion, the early 19th century had seen a tremendous increase in European interest in the land of the pharaohs. Egyptian fashions and designs flourished, and architects were eager to experiment with designs based on the wonderful illustrations in *Description de l'Égypte* (a monumental series of French publications from 1809–29). Egyptian Hall, Piccadilly, London, designed by Peter Robinson and constructed in 1812, became Britain's first complete building in the Egyptian style. Sadly, it was demolished in 1905.

Penzance mineralogist John Lavin (1796–1856) wanted a suitably fashionable place to serve as a shop and a museum in which to display his collections. After purchasing a plot on Chapel Street in 1835, Lavin decided to commission an architect to design the building in an Egyptian style, taking Robinson's Egyptian Hall as a template. Although there is no firm evidence proving that Robinson was the architect of the Egyptian House, it seems very likely since he had worked before on Cornish projects, including Trelissick House in 1825.

The Egyptian House turned out to be remarkably similar in appearance to the old Egyptian Hall. Three storeys high, its façade has ornate lotus columns, beautifully stylised cornices, eagles, lions and other authentic Egyptian details including the pylon shape, cavetto mouldings and Amon sundisks. Atop the central grand window can be found the royal coat of arms of George III and William IV. Its garish colours shriek oriental opulence, and it has been likened to an extravagant iced cake. Aside from having a ground floor that is divided in two by a recessed central doorway and vestibule, its interior is of a pretty standard Regency layout.

John Lavin lived in the upstairs part of the house, while his rock and mineral collection took up the ground floor. The collection was later sold by his son Edward to Baroness Coutts, who eventually donated it to the Oxford University Museum. By the 1960s the building had fallen into disrepair, prompting the Landmark Trust to purchase it in 1968; by 1973 the Egyptian House had been restored to its original glory. Or had it?

It had been thought that the building's extravagant embellishments were constructed of a valuable artificial material called Coade stone, popular during the period for its quality and workability. However, restorations during 2012 saw decades of thick paintwork peeled back from some of the ornamentation to reveal that the original construction material was not Coade stone. Instead, the Egyptian House is likely to be the only building west of London to have used Parker's Cement, a pioneering material made in Kent in the late 1700s. The building's beautiful embellishments have now been returned to their former glory, and are sure to turn heads as much in the 21st century as they have ever done in the past.

WILLIAM BURNS THE CAKES

1838

On the morning of 18 May 1838 the peace of Kennall Vale –
a hidden valley nestling between Redruth and Falmouth – was rudely
disrupted by an almighty explosion. People for many miles around
were startled by the sound of a massive blast that shook the earth.
Although it gave locals a shock, it came as no surprise to them when
they saw its origin – the Kennall Vale gunpowder mills. The
explosion, whose precise cause was never ascertained, caused five
mills to blow up in rapid succession.

Within a few minutes the gates of the factory were besieged by a
large crowd, all dreading that the news would be of the worst possible
kind. As the villagers congregated women shrieked and fainted and
children cried bitterly. It was found that the upper presshouse, a
building used for compressing the gunpowder into cakes, had been
utterly demolished. Only one man, William Dunstan, was known
to be at work within the building at the time of the explosion and
another, James Paddy, was engaged with a horse and cart taking
powder to and from the building.

Paddy was found lying in a watercourse about 15 yards from the
front of the building. His face and hands were severely burned and
cut, and both his right leg and arm were broken. Conscious when
found, he stated that the last thing he remembered while backing
his cart to the door of the building was a blinding flash. Paddy's
horse had been lobbed a short distance; although pretty singed,
he'd survived with just a minor cut. As for Dunstan, the first sign of
his fate was the discovery of his severed leg some distance from the
building; the rest of his mangled body was later found under a bank
30 yards away.

Established in 1811 by Benjamin Sampson to supply the
burgeoning Cornish mining and quarrying industries, the Kennall

Vale explosive mills had found instant commercial success and rapidly expanded to become a major business. The explosion proved to be only a minor setback, such was the demand for its products. The business began to decline, however, as a result of the invention of gelignite and dynamite in the late 19th century, and its operations ceased at the start of the Great War in 1914. Now managed as a nature reserve by Cornwall Wildlife Trust, Kennall Vale is a fascinating and eerie place to visit. Of course, talks of hauntings among the ruins of the once-busy gunpowder factory abound – ghost hunters find the place a real blast.

A GRUESOME MURDER
1844

Penhale Farm lies near St Breward on the western edge of Bodmin Moor. In 1844 it was owned and run by widow Phillipa Peter and her son John, assisted by long-standing employee Matthew Weeks and domestic servant Charlotte Dymond.

Weeks was short in stature and lame in his right leg; with a face that had been ravaged by severe acne, heavy brows and a certain absence of teeth, he was not the most handsome chap in Cornwall. Nevertheless, he was well thought of and performed his duties at the farm competently enough. Dymond, 18 years old, very pretty and of a flirtatious nature, had come to the farm with a considerable amount of emotional baggage. It's not known who her real parents were, but it was rumoured that her mother had threatened to kill her if she returned home. Dymond had been seeing Weeks prior to her commencing work at Penhale; she was no doubt taking advantage of the fact that he had recently come into a little money.

Charlotte Dymond was last seen in the company of Weeks on 14 April 1844, walking together at the edge of the moor. Dymond failed to return that evening, and when questioned, Weeks insisted that the two had parted early that day; he revealed that Dymond had gone to take up another position at Blisland, ten miles away. His story grudgingly accepted, work went on at Penhale as usual.

A week after Dymond had disappeared, Weeks took sudden leave of the farm. An alert was raised and the moor was searched. It didn't take the search party very long to find Dymond's body, lying face upwards beside a stream on the slopes of Roughtor. Her throat had been deeply cut from ear to ear.

Weeks was finally apprehended in Plymouth; it appears that he had intended to disappear to the Channel Islands. At his trial in Bodmin that August it took the jury just half an hour's deliberation to find him guilty of murder, and he was hanged at Bodmin Jail a few days later. A memorial column, erected by public subscription soon after the event, marks the site of Charlotte Dymond's grisly murder. It goes without saying that the place has a reputation for ghostly goings-on.

2.7 BILLION MILES FROM CORNWALL

1846

Lidcot Farm near the sleepy little village of Laneast, six miles west of Launceston, doesn't appear to be the kind of place to have produced one of the 19th century's greatest mathematicians. But it was here, in 1819, that John Couch Adams was born – a true genius with numbers, and one whose work would very nearly lead to the discovery of the planet Neptune. 'Very nearly' was to cause quite an international controversy, as we shall see.

The oldest of seven children, Adams far preferred reading to working on the family farm and demonstrated a keen interest in the universe from an early age. One childhood amusement involved marking the noon shadow of the sun throughout the year, an activity that (believe it or not) reveals that the Earth moves faster in its orbit around the sun during the winter than in summer. He often made his way across to the nearby ancient stone cross on Laneast Downs and gazed up at the starry skies, deep in meditation on the immensity of the universe.

Adams possessed an extraordinary mathematical talent, yet his family were poor tenant farmers. Luckily, the boy's education was furthered at the hamlet of Landulph near Plymouth by his mother's cousin, the Revd John Couch Grylls, from where in 1835 he observed Halley's Comet. Not only did Adams continue to observe the night skies but he set about making his own astronomical calculations and predictions of coming celestial events. He accurately calculated local times for an annular eclipse of the sun as seen from his family home at Lidcot Farm – no mean feat in an era when all calculations needed to be done with brain, pencil and paper.

The Adams' family fortunes improved when his mother inherited her aunt's estate at Badharlick, allowing John to enter Cambridge University, where he established himself as an outstanding mathematician. Continuing his fascination with the heavens, Adams used his skills to address one of the greatest problems facing astronomers at the time – the growing reluctance of the planet Uranus to obey the gravitational laws set down 150 years earlier by Isaac Newton.

Unknown to Adams, the French mathematician and astronomer Urbain Le Verrier had been working on the very same problem. Both were convinced that Uranus' path was being influenced by the gravitational pull of a large unknown planet further out from the sun. But where did their calculations suggest that this planet was and, once its position was known, who would be first to actually see it through the telescope? National pride was at stake.

In February 1844 George Airy, Astronomer Royal, learned of Adams' work on the problem and implemented a search for the planet. But Le Verrier had stolen a march on the English astronomers. On 23 September 1846 Johann Galle at the Berlin Observatory, working under Le Verrier's instructions, discovered Neptune through the observatory's nine-inch refractor. Incredibly, the planet was within just one degree of its predicted position. It shone too dimly to be seen with the unaided eye, and even through the telescope appeared as an incredibly small, pale-blue disk.

Neptune's discovery has traditionally been credited to both Le Verrier and Adams. The fourth largest and most distant planet in the solar system, it is a gas giant made up mainly of hydrogen and helium and measuring 30,775 miles across at its equator. The International Astronomical Union (IAU) have also honoured John Couch Adams with a 41-mile diameter crater on the moon, named asteroid 1996 Adams after him and officially designated the outermost ring of Neptune the Adams Ring. Not bad for a Cornish farm boy.

A LUNATIC'S WIT
1850

William Hicks was born in Bodmin on 1 April 1808. Although he was certainly no fool – becoming Governor of the County Lunatic Asylum, Bodmin, in 1848 – his wit and humour, revealed in his countless anecdotes, became extremely popular among Cornish society. Indeed, in 1893 a book titled *The Tales and sayings of W.R. Hicks* was written by William Collier.

After his appointment at Bodmin Asylum, he instituted sweeping changes that replaced the old barbarous system of treating the insane through cruel confinement to a more gentle, relaxed and humane approach. Remarkably good results followed.

One unfortunate inmate named Daniel, who had been chained up in a cell for twenty years, was considered a high-risk, dangerous lunatic. After having talked at length with the prisoner, Hicks perceived that he was, in fact, a very shrewd and witty character as incapable of harming others as he was himself. Hicks released Daniel from his bonds and struck up an excellent relationship with him. One gentleman on a visit remarked: ' I hear, man, that you are Hicks' fool.'

'Aw,' replied Daniel, 'I zee you do your own business in that line.'

On another occasion Daniel was sitting on the asylum wall watching a circus procession proceed on the way to the nearby turnpike. As the circus manager went by Daniel asked him how much he paid for each 'spekkady boss' (piebald horse) to cross the turnpike, to which the answer was the same as for each of the other horses. Daniel smiled. 'Do 'ee now?' he said. 'Well, to be sure my father 'ad a spekkady boss that never paid no turnpike. Them spekkady bosses don't pay no turnpikes here.'

'Bless my life,' said the manager, 'I am much obliged to you for informing me of the fact. So, sir, I am to understand that piebald horses are exempt from paying at the tollgate?'

'What I zed I bides by. Spekkady bosses never pay no turnpikes here in Cornwall. What they may do elsewhere, I can't zay.'

After reaching the turnpike, Daniel enjoyed watching a lively altercation between the manager and the toll-taker. Soon, the latter came galloping back, hot, flustered and angry. 'What the devil do you mean by telling me that in Cornwall piebald horses pay no turnpike?' he demanded.

Stepping back over the wall, Daniel smiled. 'Right it is,' he replied, 'they 'orses don't pay toll. No, it's you who have to pay toll for 'em.'

The Cornwall County Asylum became known as St Lawrence's Hospital in 1949 under the newly-formed NHS, at its peak providing care for 760 patients. The old asylum buildings, dating between 1815 and 1884, are still standing, but they have been empty for a number of years. The site is locked down and patrolled by security – perhaps, like Bodmin Jail, it will be renovated at some point in the future and turned into a museum.

DUCHY AND CROWN
1858

The Duchy of Cornwall owns the land of Cornwall – as soon as you cross back east of the Tamar you're back on Crown soil. But what about Cornwall's shoreline? Who owns that? After years of bitter legal wrangling, the Foreshore Case of 1858 saw the Duchy challenge the Crown over ownership of Cornwall's foreshore. Sir George Harrison, Attorney General of the Duchy, convinced the court to rule that Cornwall was 'extra-territorial' to England, while it was acknowledged to be a part of Britain.

You might wonder whether it matters if the beach you're sunning yourself on belongs to the monarch or the Duke of Cornwall, but the real significance was in who owned the mineral rights beneath the shore. So the next time you're enjoying a Cornish beach, note that you're treading on Duchy property, whereas the rest of Britain's foreshore belongs to the Crown. You can cross, unhindered, from one to the other, at the peaceful little cove on the Cornwall-Devon border at the trickling outlet of the River Marsland on the north coast, west of the Cornish village of Gooseham. You'd hardly notice the difference between one side of the beach and the other.

MOONING AROUND
1870

Throughout the ages the moon has held a special fascination for humanity. It has been the inspiration for countless myths and legends in all cultures, and our satellite has been a source of magical powers for pagan priest, shaman and witch alike.

Cornwall developed its own idiosyncratic lunar myths. One of the most famous and often-practised Cornish cures involves a remedy for warts. Today we see warts as a generally irritating, unsightly but largely benign condition, but in ancient times they were viewed as being manifestations of deeper physical or psychical problems. Getting rid of warts was the responsibility of the 'wart charmer', a physician who specialised in magical cures.

Once a closely guarded secret, some of the physical remedies used to rid the body of warts have since been revealed. One cure was to allow the rays of the full moon to shine upon a dry metal basin, and then after filling it with water bathe the part of the body affected by the warts, repeating these words: 'I wash my hands in this thy dish, O man in the moon, do grant my wish, And come and take away this'. If this failed to work, maybe you'd not caught enough moonlight, so perhaps another method might do the trick: take an unopened pod containing nine peas, rub it on the warts and while discarding it say, 'Wart, wart, dry away'. Exactly how you'd determine the number of peas inside the pod without opening it first isn't explained.

An old Cornish belief had it that a child born in the dark of the moon (at new moon) was not expected to live very long – why they should have come to think this is a mystery. Another notion was that if childbirth took place when the moon was waxing (between new moon and full), the mother's next child would be of the same sex; if the moon was waning (from full moon to new), her next child would be of the opposite sex.

A great reliance upon the supernatural power of the moon is held by practitioners of witchcraft and pagan rites, from its role in daily devotions, through its inclusion in specific magical rites for various needs, to fixed annual celebratory and devotional rites in the coven. During its two-week waxing phase the moon is said to have the power to make things grow, to empower and encourage people and things, to promote creation and achieve desires. In its waning phase, the moon's powers lean towards the dark side, and it is an especially good time for generating curses. In Cornwall, the practice of performing a curse is known as 'owl blinking'.

Cornish witches amplify the power of the moon through 'The Bucca', a local deity of the weather and tidal forces, thought to have originated as the ancient Cornish sea god. Folklore tells us that he was associated with a strange booming noise often heard in Mount's Bay before the onset of a storm. Bucca has Cornish roots far older than modern witchcraft. Having an occupation so prone to the whims of the elements, men of the sea are naturally superstitious folk. Fishermen in Newlyn, Mousehole and Penzance used to set aside three fish from their catch as an offering to Bucca, the creator of storms. A full moon that took place on a Saturday was known as the Sailor's Curse, and one proverb goes: 'A Saturday's change brings the boat to the door, but a Sunday's change brings't upon the mid floor'.

'Duffy and the Bucca' is a famous old Cornish folk story concerning an altogether different type of Bucca – actually two of them, the evil land devil Bucca Dhu and Bucca Gwidden, the spirit of light. The Devil himself is said never to be able to cross into Cornwall as he is blocked by the River Tamar, but at full moon he is capable of dispatching the hobgoblin Bucca Dhu to ride the Cornish moors accompanied by his pack of flame-eyed hounds. This horrible, hell-raising wild bunch is sometimes known as the 'Devil and his Dandy Dogs' or 'Dando and his Dogs'.

Writer William Bottrell (1816–91) published three volumes of traditional Cornish tales and legends between 1870 and 1880. In one of them he described the Bucca: 'The old people spoke of a Bucka Gwidden and a Bucka Dhu – by the former they meant good god, and by the latter an evil one, now known as Bucka boo'.

So maybe that's where the word 'bugaboo' for bogeyman originates? Curiously, there's now a popular children's television programme called *Bookaboo*, its eponymous character being a 'world-famous rock puppy and legendary canine drummer'. I wonder whether his eyes are aflame at full moon? Perhaps it's best not to let the kids know.

MORGAWR
1876

One pleasant, calm autumn evening in 1944, the fishing smack *Ibis* left Mevagissey Harbour, bound for pilchard grounds off Fowey Point. On board were Percy Hunkin, owners Eddie, Archie and Dick Lakeman, and 13-year-old Ed Boddaert (from whose account this story is taken). The sea was as smooth as glass with a slight swell. The vessel soon reached its destination but the initial catch was poor. Whales were spotted in the sea nearby – they were familiar enough. Suddenly the dark sea parted a few feet to starboard, and to everyone's astonishment and terror an object some three to four feet in diameter with a ball-like head came straight out of the water and rose to an estimated twelve feet above the water's surface, towering above the deck of the *Ibis*. The thing paused for a moment, gave out a rasping sound and then slipped vertically back under the sea. The fishermen had never before seen its like, and they instantly abandoned the idea of looking for any more pilchard.

This is one of many reports of a creature called Morgawr (Cornish, meaning 'Sea Giant'), sightings of which go back to 26 April 1876 when fishermen near Portscatho, Gerrans Bay, encountered a serpentine creature about 500 yards from shore. According to a report in the *Royal Cornwall Gazette*:

> Upon their near approach, it lifted its head and showed signs of defiance, upon which they struck it forcibly with an oar, which so far disabled it as to allow them to proceed with their work, after which they observed the serpent floating about near the boat. They pursued and captured it, bringing it ashore yet alive for exhibition, soon after which it was killed on the rocks and most inconsiderately cast

again into the sea. Why was not the wonderful creature, for which so many people have been looking, preserved and exhibited? It would have brought fame to Portscatho and riches to its captors.

In 1906 a similar creature was sighted off Land's End by two officers and a passenger on a transatlantic liner, and many similar reports of a large creature off the coast of Cornwall can be found in the press throughout much of the 20th century.

Morgawr returned to Cornish seas with a vengeance in September 1975, when Mrs Scott and Mr Riley at Pendennis Point saw a hideous humped creature with a long, bristled neck and 'stumpy horns' catch a conger eel in its mouth. There were a tremendous number of sightings during the following year, one of the most notable instances taking place in July, 25 miles south of Lizard Point, where fishermen John Cock and George Vinnicombe claim to have seen a black-bodied, grey-headed creature with an estimated length of 22 feet, which reared its neck four feet up in the water.

The most noteworthy recent report of Morgawr comes from Gerrans Bay in 1999, when John Holmes captured his sighting of an unidentified sea creature on video. Holmes' attention was caught by a movement about 250 yards off shore, and suddenly there appeared a snakelike head and neck which seemed to be raised out of the water by about three feet. He claims to have been so shocked by what he witnessed that he almost fell off the craggy rock on which he was standing.

HEROES OF THE DCLI
1881

In 1881 the Cornwall Regiment of Foot merged with the South Devonshire Regiment of Foot to become the Duke of Cornwall's Light Infantry (DCLI). The regiment saw 78 years of service to monarch and country – its last commanding officer being Major General David Tyacke (1915–2010) – prior to amalgamation with the Somerset Light Infantry in 1959 to become the Somerset and Cornwall Light Infantry.

There was nothing light about the chaps of the DCLI. No fewer than eight of its soldiers earned the highest decoration for bravery in the field, the Victoria Cross. On 10 January 1904 at a conflict at Jidballi, British Somaliland, 25-year-old Lieutenant Leslie Smith and a medical officer attempted to rescue a hospital assistant who was wounded. Under heavy fire the MO was injured and the hospital assistant was killed. Smith then attempted to bring out the wounded officer, but after helping him onto a horse, the horse was killed, the same thing happening after securing a mule. Though the medical officer sadly died, Smith stayed with him to the end, all the while fending off the enemy with his revolver. Smith survived, and finished his army career a brigadier general. Bandsman Thomas Rendle, 29, received his VC while attending to the wounded and rescuing a number of injured men from beneath rubble-strewn trenches at Wulverghem, Belgium, on 20 November 1914.

On 23 April 1951, during the Battle of Imjin, Korea, 24-year-old Lieutenant Philip Curtis made two single-handed charges on an enemy position while his platoon was under severe fire and grenade attack, and was killed during the second charge within a few yards of his objective; his last action in life was to throw a grenade, which successfully destroyed the position. The VCs of all three men are on display at the DCLI Museum at Bodmin.

Originally assigned to the DCLI, but later transferred to the Royal Dublin Fusiliers, Cornishman Sergeant Horace Curtis won the VC for his gallantry in action near Le Cateau, France in October 1918. While attacking an enemy position, Curtis's platoon came under unexpected withering fire from six machine guns. Realising that the entire platoon faced certain death unless the machine guns were taken out, Curtis unhesitatingly rushed forward into the enemy fire, somehow dodging the bullets to destroy the teams of two of the guns. His action caused the remaining four guns to surrender. But he wasn't quite finished. On noticing that a train-load of enemy troops was disembarking nearby, he single-handedly rushed them and captured more than 100 German soldiers before his comrades joined him. His VC was presented by King George V at Buckingham Palace. Following the First World War Curtis joined the DCLI Territorial Battalion at St Columb, Cornwall. This bravest of all brave Cornishmen died in Redruth in 1968, aged 77.

RAINING SNAILS
1886

Cornwall had enjoyed a beautiful summer's morning and afternoon on 8 July 1886. Late afternoon, however, saw a distinct blackening of the skies, as ever-darker clouds rolled in from the west and the temperature plummeted. Then came the rain, in pulsing waves that swept across the county, and soon the thunder began to rumble. In Redruth at the height of the storm came another sound – a pitter-pattering like hail – but this was no common sky-fall. From beneath umbrellas, bay windows and shop fronts, residents of the town were astonished to see masses of small snails descend from the heavens. Those caught out in the open had no option but to crunch their way over the creatures, so thickly did they cover the ground. The roads and fields were strewn with them over a distinct area of around half a square mile.

The shower of snails lasted for about ten minutes, while the storm itself gradually petered out. On closer inspection the snails – all alive – seemed to be quite different in appearance from those common to the district. Those who hadn't witnessed the remarkable incident were content to mock the reports. One newspaper correspondent said that he had heard of the supposed fall of snails, and likened them to 'witch stories'; he was astonished that any newspaper of such 'great and deserved repute' as the *Redruth Independent* should ever print such an absurd story.

Yet there seems no doubt that there had actually been a fall of snails. Other correspondents to the *Independent* recounted their own experiences during the deluge of gastropods, including one who, thinking they might be sea snails, found that they survived when placed in saltwater. Another correspondent, thinking the snails had a terrestrial origin, tried the same experiment and found that they died in brine. So the mystery of their origin remains.

Perhaps the ancient 'Snail Creep' dance and ceremony of the Rescorla Festival, in which a musical band marches leading a long procession of couples around in a spiral, led by two people holding up branches (the snail's eyestalks) harkens back to a distant memory of a similar rain of snails over Cornwall in medieval times?

THE EIGHTH PLAGUE
1895

Until 1895, no juvenile locust had ever been recorded in Great Britain. Then, during a balmy spell on 8 and 9 October, locusts appeared in large numbers across Cornwall and other places in the west of the UK. In the *Journal of the Plymouth Institute* an entomologist wrote that he had never heard of a previous visit to England by this insect – indeed, it appears that this particular species had never been seen before anywhere in Europe. *The Monthly Magazine of Entomology* reported that these locusts were new to European fauna, and were not mentioned in any reference work on European orthoptera.

This appears to have been the only recorded case of a locust swarm in England, but other animals have been accused of acting like locusts across the county of Cornwall. In February 2011 the local media compared the sudden arrival of vast flocks of starlings to swarms of locusts. The unusually large numbers of the birds arriving from the Continent was caused by a particularly cold spell of weather in Europe. Farmers in Cornwall demanded that they be allowed to use their shotguns because, like locusts, the starlings were eating their way relentlessly through copious quantities of valuable animal feed. It was a no-go on this option, because starlings are on the environmental red list, their population as a whole having fallen by more than half since 1970 according to the Royal Society for the Protection of Birds.

Some people took to walking around beneath umbrellas, so frequently did the white stuff fall from the sky. The Trevelgue Holiday Park in Newquay was faced with a bill of £10,000 to clean up the enormous mess of droppings left by a flock of millions of the birds. Trevelgue's Mike Finnigan said: 'The bird droppings are causing a major problem. It's acidic and the sheer quantity is phenomenal. The roads on the campsite are absolutely covered and the trees and caravans are lagged. It's taking major branches off some trees because of the sheer weight. In some places it's up to seven inches deep. I have worked here for fifteen years and I've never seen anything like it.'

Later that year headlines of more unwelcome marauders appeared in the Cornish media. This particular plague consisted of criminals intent on plundering the county's unprotected metalwork – thefts of all kinds of metal had seen a huge rise during the year because of a global surge in the market price. In response, Devon and Cornwall Police established Operation Galvin. Its purpose, according to Inspector Mark Richards, was to undertake an investigation into 'teams of rural criminals who, like locusts, are stripping the county bare of metal'.

Examples of the desperate lengths to which Cornish metal-locusts were prepared to go include a forest-based gang whose gatherings around the camp fire would burn the plastic off stolen cables containing copper wire, and a thief who was found dead beneath the abandoned St Lawrence's Hospital in Bodmin while stripping out its wires – he had electrocuted himself with his own power tools.

Newquay Zoo is the place to go to see real locusts. I'm not sure if they have any on display by themselves, but hundreds of the creatures daily form the basis of many of the animals' meals – collectively they enjoy chomping through about a quarter of a ton of locusts each year.

THE MYSTERY OF
THE *MOHEGAN*
1898

For millennia, mariners have recognised that the hazards to be found around Cornwall and the Isles of Scilly make them among the most treacherous coastlines in the world. 'Treacherous' certainly applies to the Manacles off the Lizard near Porthoustock, for this small group of rocks is said to be the graveyard of a thousand ships. Two large communal graves in the churchyard of St Keverne attest to the awful wrecking power of the Manacles, two miles to the east. One contains bodies from the 1855 wreck of the *John*, a ship full of emigrants bound for Quebec, the other is full of the remains of the passengers and crew of the New York-bound liner the SS *Mohegan*, which ran aground in 1898. Even today, the latter disaster is spoken about in hushed terms by some elderly locals, whose parents and grandparents bore witness to the great loss of life.

Built for 'safety at sea' and rated A1 by Lloyds of London, the *Mohegan* was a brand new passenger liner/cattle transport that had originally been named 'Cleopatra' by the owners of the Atlantic Transport Line. *Cleopatra* sailed on her maiden voyage from London to New York in the summer of 1898, but all was not well from the outset. Disconcertingly, the ship was noticed to have many defects and blame was laid at the rush with which it had been built in Hull. Following extensive repairs and a sea trial, the Board of Trade passed the vessel as seaworthy. In order to avoid unnecessary publicity links with the maiden voyage fiasco, the 475ft-long ship was renamed *Mohegan*.

Embarking on her 'second' maiden voyage to New York and under the command of Captain Richard Griffith, the *Mohegan* left Tilbury Docks on 13 October 1898, and after calling at Dover on the same evening, proceeded westwards along the English Channel. Hitting her maximum speed of 13 knots and keeping close to the coast, the *Mohegan* neared Cornwall on the evening of 14 October. A wrong bearing had been noticed by some of the crew, who saw that the Eddystone Lighthouse was too distant and the coast perilously close. Nearing the entrance of Falmouth Harbour, she turned southwest towards the mouth of the Helford Estuary, maintaining the same top rate of knots. Coastguards at Coverack signalled the ship with warning rockets – but to no avail. The *Mohegan* maintained her course, seemingly oblivious to the disaster that was sure to come. At Porthoustock near the Manacles, those on shore watched in horror as the liner, lights ablaze, ran full speed towards the rocks. James Hill, cox of the Porthoustock lifeboat, roused his crew, crying, 'She's coming right in!'

Too late, the crew of the *Mohegan* stopped her engines, but momentum carried her forward to a crunching encounter with the Manacles which tore the ship's hull apart. Captain Griffith's earlier modification to the lifeboat rails prevented them from being swung out rapidly enough, and only two were launched. Twelve minutes after impact, the *Mohegan* sank, her mast and funnels remaining above water. While the lifeboat *Charlotte* saved 44 lives, 106 souls were lost.

Captain Griffith and his officers are supposed to have gone down with the ship, but there remains a nagging suspicion among locals that the captain survived. Several independent witnesses reported seeing a figure in brown overalls jump from the side of the *Charlotte* as it landed on the beach at Porthoustock and bolt off through the village 'as if fired from a gun'. Early next morning a man fitting that description was seen taking a boat and rowing across the River Helford. Nobody was able to establish the man's identity – he was never seen again, and the body of Griffith was never recovered.

How the *Mohegan* became so hopelessly lost, given all the signals and warnings, has never been satisfactorily answered. Captain Griffith knew the area well, and rumours circulated that he had deliberately crashed the ship under some clandestine deal with the Atlantic Transport Company.

The last body washed up on shore eight weeks later. Meanwhile, large quantities of beer carried on board the *Mohegan* also found their way onto Cornish beaches – it was apparently of good quality and thoroughly appreciated by the locals.

SKIRTING WITH IDENTITY
1901

Following a career of gallant war service in the late 19th century, the flamboyant Liskeard-born Louis Duncombe-Jewell found himself increasingly drawn towards issues of Cornish identity. In 1901 he was instrumental in founding the Cornish Celtic Society and at a meeting of the Pan-Celtic Congress (a cultural organisation promoting the Celtic languages) he made a passionate plea for Cornwall to be recognised as a Celtic nation.

In the following year he discovered proof – in the form of early 16th-century carvings on benches at Altarnun Church showing bagpipe-wielding minstrels – that plain kilts were worn by men in Cornwall in ages past. Taking this idea forward, he proudly sported a woad-blue kilt at the Pan-Celtic Congress of 1903. Perhaps impressed by Duncombe-Jewell's attire, his enthusiasm, or a combination of both, the 1904 Congress saw Cornwall join Ireland, Scotland, Wales, the Isle of Man and Brittany as a recognised member of the Celtic family.

Although the Cornish Celtic Society folded with the outbreak of the Great War, he was to help found the Cornish Gorsedd, an organisation that still exists to promote the Celtic spirit and identity of Cornwall in the United Kingdom.

A desire for the increased recognition of Cornish identity blossomed after the Second World War, and in 1963 E. E. Morton Nance, the Bard of Padstow, designed a Cornish national tartan. Eschewing the plain dark tartans then being worn by Cornish patriots, Nance considered tartan to be the heritage of all Celts, and he celebrated Cornish identity by giving relevance to each of its colours. White on black represents St Piran's flag (patron saint of Cornwall, and of tinners); black and gold acknowledges the colours of the ancient Cornish kings; red is for the beak and legs of the chough (the Cornish national bird) and blue is for the seas surrounding Cornwall. It's a striking design, quite unmistakable owing to the prominent St Piran's cross.

Since then eight more Cornwall-related tartans have been registered, and you're likely to see them on display, whether as part of a shop display or on items of clothing (including kilts), any time you're out and about in Truro on a busy day. With regard to kilts, it is not known what the convention on undergarments is.

THE FALL GUY
1911

On the afternoon of 25 July 1911, 53-year-old Cornishman Bobby Leach climbed into a 7ft-long riveted steel drum at Navy Island, upstream of Niagara Falls. The peculiar-looking vessel took 18 minutes to reach the edge of the Horseshoe Falls, the largest of the three falls that make up Niagara, before being swept over the 174ft-high cataract. Twenty-two minutes later, the vessel, stuck in the river at the base of the falls, was recovered and hauled to shore. Removing the small, tight lid from the battered vessel, rescuers peered inside to find that the man had survived. He had suffered two broken kneecaps and a fractured jaw.

Ten years before, 63-year-old Annie Taylor had been the first to accomplish this most dangerous of extreme sports. While Taylor had survived with just a cut to her face, the plummet over the famous Falls did Leach far more damage. Having boasted that 'anything Annie could do, he could do better', his injuries cost him a six-month spell in hospital.

Bobby Leach – the first *man* to survive the falls – did, however, manage to capitalise on his insane Niagara escapade far better than Taylor. He embarked on a tour of Canada, the United States and England, regaling audiences at music halls and lecture halls with his story and posing for photographs beside his vessel (always described as a barrel, but in truth it was nothing like the real wooden barrel in which Taylor had braved the Falls).

Going over Niagara Falls had been the final item in a 'Niagara triple challenge' that Leach had boasted of being able to complete. Three years before, he had base-jumped off the Upper Steel Arch Bridge (known as the 'Honeymoon Bridge') at Niagara and parachuted to the shore below. The second challenge was completed in the summer of 1910 when he made a trip in his 7ft 'barrel' through the Great Gorge Rapids and the Niagara Whirlpool downstream of the bridge. During this episode the stabilising anchor to the vessel had become detached and he became stuck in the maelstrom, falling unconscious. Leach was rescued by William Hill, who bravely swam the vicious waters and steered both victim and the barrel to safety through the lower rapids. Within a few weeks Leach had made three successful navigations of the rapids and whirlpool.

Addicted to the adulation and publicity resulting from such daredevil actions, Leach returned to Niagara Falls in 1920 and made several parachute jumps from an aeroplane over the Falls. In 1926, while on a publicity tour in New Zealand, Leach succumbed to the common comedic joke of slipping on a banana skin. Having injured his leg, an infection set in, followed by gangrene and septicaemia. He died two months later.

Cornwall itself has plenty of dramatic scenery, and the steep, crumbly cliffs at Pentargon near Boscastle host the county's highest waterfall, a 120ft-high cataract that was famously written about by Thomas Hardy. Nobody knows precisely where in Cornwall Bobby Leach was born in 1858, but it would be fitting and appropriate if this famous Cornishman – the first man to brave the Niagara Falls – came from somewhere nearby.

IDEALS AND VILE DEALS
1915

A few miles west along the coast from St Ives can be found Higher Tregerthen, a cluster of large houses set among grey rocks near Zennor. It was in this isolated place that controversial author D. H. Lawrence attempted to find a little peace and privacy. His recently published novel, *The Rainbow*, had been severely mauled by critics and banned by the Bow Street Magistrates for its blunt treatment of sexual desire and its anti-war overtones: hardly surprising, considering that it was 1915, and Europe was engaged in the most vicious war in history. Peace and privacy was a romantic luxury that few but the most privileged or deluded could expect to attain.

Along with his new wife Frieda and fellow writers and pacifists Katherine Mansfield and John Middleton Murry, Lawrence settled in Higher Tregerthen. Their common ambition to escape from the limelight initially succeeded, and before long they set about creating an ideal community called 'Rananim'. They were later joined in a neighbouring cottage by like-minded composer Peter Warlock, along with his girlfriend 'Puma' (artists' model Minnie Channing). Lawrence began his next novel, *Women in Love*, while at the same time starting an intimate relationship with William Hocking, his new near-neighbour at Lower Tregerthen Farm.

This idyllic scene of peace, love and freedom, set against the gruesome backdrop of global conflict, would not last very long – after all, Rananim's initiators were all artists of an unusual and individualistic bent, a group whose inclination towards *behaving* like a group can be likened to an attempt to herd cats. Even had they gelled, had the arguments between them been settled amicably, and even if egos and personalities had not been so abrasive, it's pretty certain that Rananim would have failed anyway.

At the height of the Great War, every community across the land had been affected by the wanton slaughter in the trenches. It comes as no surprise to learn that the sudden appearance of such an apparently carefree Bohemian group amid the close-knit community of Zennor was resented from the outset; the strangers' attitude conveyed a deep disrespect for the suffering of the times. Moreover, each of Rananim's members were preceded by a hefty baggage of scandal and intrigue. They were not liked and not wanted. Before long, rumours that the group was sympathetic towards the enemy, the Central Powers of Germany and Austria-Hungary, turned into outright accusations of spying and signalling to U-boats prowling off the Cornish coast. There was certainly a good reason to think this might be so: Lawrence's wife, Frieda, was a cousin of Manfred von Richthofen, the infamous ace fighter known as the Red Baron.

Accused of showing lights to submarine crews, Rananim and its founders were investigated by the police and their cottages searched. Despite finding no damning evidence, and after ransacking Lawrence's belongings and destroying some of his 'utterly filthy' work, they were ordered to leave Cornwall, which they did in October 1917. The experience left Lawrence with a bitter taste in his mouth and an antipathy towards his fellow countrymen, detesting the small-mindedness of the Cornish people. He was to write about the episode in his 1923 novel, *Kangaroo*, in a chapter appropriately entitled 'The Nightmare'.

MYLOR'S BLACK BULL
1928

Stories of the paranormal arise from a variety of sources. Some appear to be anchored firmly in well-established ancient folklore and superstition. Others seem, on face value, to have a ring of historically deep authenticity, but closer research reveals a source that is located in relatively recent times. Such is the case of the 'Black Bull of Mylor', a story that has gained a great deal of prominence among paranormal circles and in books, but which, despite its ghoulish appeal, can be traced to a chain of conversations.

The story was first published in a 1928 edition of the journal *Old Cornwall*, where W. D. Watson, founder member of the Old Cornwall Society, recounts a tale that had been told to him in the late 19th century by an old woman, who in turn had been young at the time of the supernatural incident. The old lady's father had been one of two coastguards who, sometime in the mid-19th century, while patrolling near Mylor Creek, were terrified by a large, thunderous, fire-snorting bull with glowing red eyes. Watson recalled the old lady's tale in detail since it had made such an impression on him:

> One night the two men were out on their rounds, and were intending to make their way towards Trefusis Point, so as to pass by the Big Zoon, when after they had passed the church stile they were suddenly brought to a stop. Away in the distance, coming towards them, they could hear a fearful roaring noise; then they could hear the gravel flying, and as the sound came nearer they could make out the form of a big black bull, tearing towards them with fire coming from his nostrils, and roaring something terrible!

They took and runned back towards the churchyard
and got in behind the wall, and when the bull passed by they
both fired their pistols right at him; but they might just so
well have spit at him for all the use it was! Anyhow, they
took on after the bull, and it kept running over the beach
below Lawithick. At last we indoors could hear the noise.
We two and the neighbour came out to see what was on,
but we went back again pretty quick! The houses were
shaking as the bull passed by, and he went away up the road
with the men after him till after passing Well Ackett, and
there they lost all sight and sound of him, and at last came
back again. The next day they sent round to the different
parishes but nobody had lost a black bull, nor heard of one
being lost!

How much of this is truth and how much is 'bull', I leave for you
to decide.

CORNWALL'S WITCH-FINDER

1930

Our knowledge of Cornwall's rich heritage of folklore and legend would be far poorer were it not for the lifetime's work of William Henry Paynter (1901–76), a Cornish antiquary and folklorist whose speciality of collecting witch stories and folklore during the inter-war years earned him the title of the 'Cornish Witch-finder'. Belief in witches and the passing-down of traditional oral folklore was on the wane during the 1920s and 30s. Paynter's painstaking attempts to gather as much of this ancient cultural narrative as he could to preserve them before they were lost forever resulted in an impressive body of work.

Born in Callington and later resident of Liskeard, Paynter travelled throughout Cornwall, collecting stories of folklore and witches at every possible opportunity from every possible source. At the Cornish Gorsedd of 1930 his work was formally recognised, and on being appointed a bard he adopted the name 'Whyler Pystry' (Cornish: 'Searcher-out of Witchcraft').

In addition, Paynter's research took him into such diverse areas as ghosts, magical charms, mermaids and beliefs attached to birds and wildlife. He founded the Callington Old Cornwall Society in 1928, a group still going today and which has inspired many other towns to set up their own local history groups. Following the war, Paynter became something of a radio and television celebrity, offering his own take on all things Cornish.

Much of Paynter's extensive lifetime collection of Cornish artefacts was placed on display at the Cornish Museum at East Looe, a museum he founded in 1959. In addition to exhibits of a folklorish and magical nature, the displays included more mundane aspects of Cornish life in bygone days, including early kitchen and lighting devices, sections on early transport, John Wesley, Cornish tin and china clay mining.

EINSTEIN BAFFLES BETTY
1933

How many people could claim to have met the greatest scientist of the 20th century, secretly witnessed the bizarre rituals of the 'wickedest man in the world', had an affair with the inventor of radio, mixed with some of the world's greatest artists, been friends with European royalty and inspired a great book?

These are just a few of the remarkable events in the life of Betty Paynter (1907–80) of Boskenna, seat of the Paynter family near St Buryan, overlooking the cliffs at St Loy Bay near Land's End.

Elizabeth Narcissa Marie Paynter had a remarkably interesting life. As an innocent 10-year-old she had inadvertently and secretly seen the infamous master of the occult Aleister Crowley holding a macabre ritual in the nearby Trevellow Woods, describing it as 'a real orgy, fit for the *News of the World.*'

Two years before Betty was born, T. E. Lawrence – later to become famous as Lawrence of Arabia – absconded from the Royal Garrison Artillery at St Mawes Castle and became smitten with Ethel Paynter, Betty's mother. According to Betty, Lawrence would roar up and down the drive of Boskenna on his motorcycle, hoping to impress. Artists were always welcome at Boskenna. Another Lawrence – author D.H.– would visit from Zennor (see also p.95–6). Post-impressionist painter Augustus John was a regular visitor, along with many of the avant-garde set of the inter-war period.

Guglielmo Marconi, the famous radio inventor, seems also to have struck up a close friendship with Ethel Paynter while testing wireless communication in Cornwall. From the experimental transmitter at Poldhu in 1924, Ethel became the first person to speak directly to Australia by radio. In the same year Marconi's marriage broke up, and he invited both Ethel and Betty to a Mediterranean cruise on his steam yacht, *Electra*. During the three-month cruise

Marconi introduced them to King Alfonso XIII of Spain and his mother Queen Maria, and King Victor Emmanuel III and Queen Elena of Italy. Marconi's passions seem to have shifted towards Betty during the voyage. After spending Christmas at Boskenna, national newspapers were predicting her imminent engagement to the great inventor, who considered her to be 'a splendid example of country girlhood'. It was not to be. Although he had been sweet and generous, and had proposed to her, Betty maintained that the age difference was too great: he was 50, and she just 17. But she moved on quickly, for in 1925 she was one of the summer débutantes presented at Court to King George V.

In 1933 Boskenna was visited by Albert Einstein during his brief stay in England after leaving Nazi Germany in 1933. The reason for the great scientist's visit to Boskenna is not recorded, but it is not beyond belief; for example, in September that year he is known to have sat for the sculptor Jacob Epstein in a beach hut in Cromer, Norfolk. While at Boskenna, the great physicist's attempts to explain his Theory of Relativity to Betty sadly proved futile. She recalled, 'I used to go boringly up to him and say, "Oh, Mr Einstein, I've forgotten what you said," and he used to start explaining all over again.' Einstein might have been a genius, but it seemed his teaching skills weren't quite up to scratch.

Following two marriages and large debts, Betty sold the increasingly financially burdensome Boskenna in the late 1950s; the estate was broken up and the farms sold off. Yet the unique atmosphere of those inter-war years at the house near the cliff lives on in Mary Wesley's best-selling novel *The Camomile Lawn* (1984) and its TV adaptation.

AN AMBITIOUS NAZI'S CORNISH DREAMS

1936

Of all the leading Nazis in Hitler's gruesome portfolio of lascivious lackeys, Teutonic toadies and flaccid Fuhrer-pleasers, one man stands out above the others – Joachim von Ribbentrop.

In November 1934, Hitler's foreign minister Ribbentrop visited Britain, where he met with a host of British artists and politicians, including George Bernard Shaw, Sir Austen Chamberlain, Lord Cecil and Lord Lothian. It was Lothian's praise for the natural friendship between Germany and Britain that caused Ribbentrop to tell his master in Berlin that all elements of British society wished for closer ties with Germany. Hitler was delighted. While other Nazis in foreign affairs said that an alliance with Britain was out of the question, Ribbentrop could be relied upon. He was a man whom Hitler praised as the only one who told him 'the truth about the world abroad'.

Ribbentrop was not such a well-liked character, not even among the high-ranking Nazis. Josef Goebbels famously remarked that Ribbentrop had 'bought his name, married his money and swindled his way into office'. Yet he shone in Hitler's eyes, and on 2 August 1936 was appointed Reich Ambassador to Britain, tasked with persuading the British Government not to get involved in Germany's so-called 'territorial disputes' and to work with them against the Soviet Union. In London, Ribbentrop proved an unmitigated disaster. Prone to fits of rage directed towards anyone he considered his social inferior, he found plenty of time to ingratiate himself into high society. He caused outrage when on his presentation to King George VI he gave a sudden Nazi salute that very nearly toppled the monarch. Touches such as posting

SS guards outside the German Embassy and flying swastikas from all official cars didn't help his case.

After winding everyone up in London, Ribbentrop was invited to stay 250 miles away as a guest of Colonel Edward Bolitho, Lord Lieutenant of Cornwall. At Bolitho's home at Trengwainton, the Nazi fell in love with Cornwall, particularly the town of St Ives on the north coast, where he delighted in the sea air and the special way that the bay is illuminated by the sun. Soon his grandiose thoughts were set in train. When the coming war with Britain had been successfully concluded, no grand residence in grey London would do for the Reich Ambassador. No, his reward was to be on Cornwall's south coast at St Michael's Mount. The St Aubyn family would be unceremoniously turfed out of their ancestral home, and the picturesque island was to be his domain. Indeed, Ribbentrop boasted that Hitler would give him Cornwall itself. Documents found in recent years have proven that many of England's gems were to be spared from bombing during the war, including St Ives. A large set of holiday postcards bought by Ribbentrop during his stay in Cornwall were used in 1942 to illustrate *Militärgeographische Angaben über England Südküste*, a top-secret German guide to the English coastline.

Ribbentrop was thrown out of the UK before the outbreak of war, but continued as the Nazi state's Minister for Foreign Affairs, choosing to work closely with the SS. He was arrested by Allied troops in May 1945 and on 16 October 1946, having been tried at Nuremberg, became the first Nazi to be hanged there.

THE CULTISH, CORNISH CONNECTIONS OF ALEISTER CROWLEY

1938

After a gap of two decades we return to Zennor, only to plunge headlong into a fascinating web of occult mystery involving a man who, in his time, was reviled as 'the wickedest man in the world': Aleister Crowley (1875–1947), the original, self-styled antichrist.

Crowley's thoughts, words and reputed deeds were antithetical to the vast majority of people in Edwardian England. His revolt against the moral and religious views of the era earned him almost unanimous detestation. His hedonistic motto 'Do what thou will shall be the whole of the law' revelled in unleashed freedom but took no heed of the rights of others. Crowley's rise (or perhaps, more appropriately, descent) to such unanimous detestation presented him with few problems; he welcomed the notoriety. After all, his own mother had labelled him 'the Beast' at an early age and he, in turn, hated her; it was the likely genesis of his appalling misogyny in later life.

Crowley's most infamous Cornish connection – yet one that has tantalisingly few corroborative details – allegedly took place in 1938 at Higher Tregerthen near Zennor, where the failed Rananim community had been based two decades before. A nearby resident, Katherine Arnold-Forster, had confronted Crowley and his group over a 'wicked incident' in which they had been involved. It presumably involved Crowley's love of conducting weird rites, conjurations and blood-sacrifices at ancient sites and churches in the area, and at least one male member of the group had become a gibbering wreck as a result. Following a fierce argument, Arnold-Forster left for home: but she never made it back. Her body was found the following day, and her death was never fully explained.

It's difficult to separate fact from fantasy in Crowley's strange life of esoteric poetry, dark magic, black rites, deeply unconventional views and debauched practices. Wild, rugged Cornwall, with its peculiar individuality and rich history of folklore, druids and magic, proved a great attraction. He made extensive visits throughout the county to fellow occultists, witches' covens and gatherings of like-minded 'eccentrics of the extreme' over a number of decades in the first half of the 20th century. At various times (sometimes with his mistress and illegitimate son) he lived in Newlyn, Bodmin, Penzance and Land's End.

In the summer of 1943, at the Men-an-Tol stone circle near Land's End, Crowley conducted a black ritual whose purpose remains shrouded in mystery. It's perhaps coincidental that the magic rite took place overlooking the Atlantic, only a few months after what the Germans called 'Black May', the turning point in the Second World War's Battle of the Atlantic, where finally more U-boats were being sunk than Allied shipping casualties. According to rumours, the cottage that had been occupied by Crowley at Land's End was later tenanted by two women; one was found dead (cause unknown) while the other was sent to the asylum, babbling incoherently that the Devil had revealed himself to her.

Reminiscent of the scandal surrounding D. H. Lawrence and Rananim, Crowley and his occult group were subject to rumours of spying and accused of spreading occult disinformation. They were even fingered as suspects in the infamous Walton Murder of 1945, a crime with overt occult overtones, which was investigated by the famous Fabian of the Yard yet never solved. Yet for all his reputation, Crowley, the 'Great Beast', was never put on trial for his involvement in the sordid underworld of the occult and his alleged crimes are perhaps more the result of his vile reputation and his own keen eye for negative self-publicity.

A CALL TO ARMS
1939

Arms: Sable fifteen Bezants in pile within a Bordure barry wavy of eight Argent and Azure.
Crest: On a Wreath Argent and Azure a Chough proper resting the dexter claw upon a Ducal Coronet Or.
Supporters: On the dexter side a Fisherman holding over the exterior shoulder a Net and on the sinister side a Miner resting the exterior hand on a Sledge Hammer all proper.
Motto: 'One and All'.

Such is the heraldic description of the official blazon of Cornwall. This latest version of the county's coat of arms dates back to 1939. Visually, it's rather distinctive, and it's unmistakeably Cornish – the tin miner and fisherman see to that. Central to the coat is a shield of waves, and central to that shield, just as the county itself is enclosed by the sea, a smaller shield bears 15 golden roundels or 'bezants'. The origin of these bold roundels, which can be seen virtually everywhere in Cornwall, from lampposts to litter bins, is rather uncertain. Earlier Cornish emblems show the bezels arranged as a shield border or arranged to fill the whole shield, as on the arms of the Duke of Cornwall, which date back to the 15th century. One story tells how King John's second son Richard, 1st Earl of Cornwall, was captured by Saracens while at the Crusades during the 1240s. It is said that loyal Cornishmen helped raise the ransom of 15 golden coins – or bezants, which take their name from Byzantium – hence their appearing on the shield to commemorate the event. Similarly, 'One and All' refers to this act of devotion to the Earl by his loyal Cornishmen. However, although Richard was involved with ransoming captured prisoners in the Holy Land, there is no record of him ever being held captive himself, so perhaps the 'bezants' will have to remain a mystery.

And how loyal was Richard to Cornwall? He had received Cornwall in 1225 on his 16th birthday from his brother, King Henry III. Although his revenues from Cornwall made Richard one of Europe's wealthiest men, it appears that he was no great fan of his earldom, for he never set foot in the county.

Sitting proudly and rather cheekily atop the Cornish coat of arms is a red-billed chough. This bird has had deep cultural connections with Cornwall through the ages. One legend tells us of King Arthur's final battle near Camelford, at a place that later became known as Slaughter Bridge. After being felled by a poisoned arrow shot by his nephew Mordred, Arthur was taken to Tintagel Castle. The knights surrounding the dying king were perturbed by a cacophony of moaning supernatural voices, as the seas whipped up and the winds blasted the castle. The ghostly lamentations eventually ceased when Arthur was finally laid to rest, to be replaced by sweet voices proclaiming that he would one day return to be King of Cornwall. A red-billed chough flew over – it was King Arthur's spirit. This event began the Cornish veneration of that particular little species of crow, and it is said that no luck follows a man who kills a Cornish chough.

AN UNUSUAL VISITOR
TO CORNWALL
1939

As grey storm clouds gathered over Europe, a vast grey battleship appeared on the horizon at Falmouth. Looming ever closer, those viewing it through binoculars could plainly see, flying from its mast, the emblem of Nazi Germany – the dreaded swastika. Yet no alarm was raised. As the vessel drew closer, no shots were fired from on-shore batteries. Despite being present in large numbers, the ships of the Royal Navy remained quiet, and in the skies there only appeared aircraft with observers curious to get a closer look. SMS *Schleswig-Holstein* – infamous for its vicious bombardment of Scarborough, Hartlepool and Whitby – came into port and moored off Carrick Roads without a single shot being fired from either side. On the contrary, Hitler's battleship was received in Cornwall with an unusually warm welcome, and on no fewer than two occasions – once in April 1938 and again in February 1939. Britain would not declare war on Germany until seven months later. The *Schleswig-Holstein*'s attacks on those defenceless English northeastern towns had taken place in December 1914, a quarter of a century earlier.

The *Schleswig-Holstein*'s visit to Falmouth took place at the conclusion of its four-and-a-half month cruise of the West Indies. Commanded by Frigattenkapitän Arnold Bentlage and with a complement of 850, she had been used for a number of years as a training ship for the Führer's budding officer cadets. Major Mercer of the Duke of Cornwall Light Infantry (DCLI) was invited aboard, where he discussed Anglo-German relations with the German officers. During dinner, Kapitän Bentlage proposed that 30 officers and seamen visit the DCLI regiment at Bodmin to play a friendly game of football.

The pride of the Fatherland's seamen arrived at the DCLI head-quarters in a large coach hired by the German Consul. Oberleutnant zur See Otto von Bülow enjoyed his first views of Cornwall and soon ingratiated himself with the regiment's men. Upon seeing a dartboard for the first time, he was told that they were used for target practice – something that greatly impressed von Bülow, little suspecting traditional English irony.

A certain Leutnant Bligh – known by his colleagues as Leutnant Meuterei (Lieutenant Mutiny) – was in charge of the German team. Following a group photograph, each member of the British team was presented with a badge, while a large framed photograph of the *Schleswig-Holstein*, signed by Kapitän Bentlage, was given to the DCLI. Despite a valiant effort in which the British scored an early first goal, the weather changed and a gale whipped up that favoured the Germans during the second half. The final result – DCLI 1, *Schleswig-Holstein* 3.

On the last day of the ship's visit, Major and Mrs Mercer, Captain and Mrs Wetherell, along with members of the Falmouth British Legion, enjoyed a lavish party aboard the German battleship, during which the British guest of honour received the 'accolade' of sitting beneath a large painting of a glowering Adolf Hitler. During the party it became clear that the Germans were all deluded into thinking their country was not responsible for the First World War. Later that evening, following warm farewells, the *Schleswig-Holstein* cast off, its men standing to attention on deck giving the Nazi salute.

On 1 September 1939 the *Schleswig-Holstein* fired the first shots of the Second World War as it shelled Polish forts on the Baltic coast. The DCLI were posted to France, taking up positions in the Maginot Line. Among the prisoners captured as that vast defensive folly was overrun in May 1940 was Lance-Corporal Harold Walford of the DCLI. During a Nazi propaganda broadcast from Berlin, Walford was interviewed and said that he had taken part in the football match against the crew of the *Schleswig-Holstein* in Bodmin.

As for the battleship, it was recommissioned in 1944, its armour and gunnery beefed up and refitted at Gotenhafen (Gdynia) on Poland's Baltic coast; before managing to leave port it was devastated by an RAF bombing raid, receiving three direct hits.

Following the war the remains of the *Schleswig-Holstein* were towed into the Gulf of Finland, where it was used for target practice and later sunk.

BLITZ BRAVERY FROM FIRST TO LAST

1940

At 2.30 p.m. on 10 July 1940 the nauseating whine of air-raid sirens filled the Cornish air. A lone Heinkel bomber of the Luftwaffe, operating from a captured airbase in Brittany, flew down the River Penryn and appeared over Falmouth. After releasing its deadly load on the docks, the enemy aircraft disappeared over the English Channel. It was Cornwall's first taste of the Blitz.

Extensive damage was suffered by Falmouth's wharves where six dock workers lost their lives, and hundreds were trapped by the raging flames. The lone German raider had scored hits on several ships. Two bombs damaged the oil tanker *British Chancellor*, killing four engineers on board, but the vessel remained afloat – fortunately it was not full of oil at the time. Hit in the fuel tank, the *Tascalusa* immediately sank. Damage was sustained by the Dutch vessel *Zwarte Zee*, while the Greek ship *Maria Chandris*, packed with cotton, burned fiercely, its crew jumping overboard.

In a remarkable act of coolly executed bravery, Captain Charles Jackson, a Falmouth Trinity House pilot (off duty at the time of the raid), cycled to the docks. Acting single-handedly, he went over to the burning wharf and had the undamaged ship *Luminetta* moved so that he could manoeuvre his tug across to the burning Greek ship. After coming alongside and boarding the *Maria Chandris*, Jackson made fast the towropes, resumed the wheel of his tug and piloted the vessel from the docks, beaching her near St Mawes. Next, with the help of Commander Austin and two naval ratings, the heroic captain did the same for the burning *British Chancellor*. While the Greek vessel was a write-off, the *British Chancellor* was later refitted and put back into service. Captain Jackson was recommended for an MBE by the Admiralty for his bravery and clear thinking.

Falmouth, along with many other militarily and strategically important places in Cornwall, continued to suffer bombing raids during the war. At one time, it had more air-raid warnings than anywhere else in the country. The last air raid took place on the night of 30 May 1944 when a sizeable force of German bombers bombed the seafront. Shops and hotels caught fire and the high-octane petrol tanks at Swanvale burned for several days, causing the evacuation of most of its residents.

A Wren named Marion Whittaker, based in Falmouth, responded to the raid with incredible bravery and initiative. The bombing started just after Whittaker had come off duty at midnight as she donned her helmet in preparation for fire-watching. One of the bombs landed near the Wren headquarters, producing a large blaze at nearby garages. Fully aware that the garages contained US Army vehicles laden with fuel and ammunition, she ventured inside to salvage the vehicles. While explosions rent the smoke-filled air around her, Whittaker helped to remove four vehicles from the inferno. She later commented that she had been too busy to be frightened. Her flag officer commended Whittaker for 'A gallant action, regardless of her own personal safety, showing an admirable combination of pluck and presence of mind'.

Later that year the heroic Wren was awarded the OBE by King George VI, a fitting reward for bravery any Cornishman or women would be proud of.

NO HANGING AROUND
1942

On Christmas Eve 1942 two police officers, Sergeant Bennett and 17-year-old cadet Eric Chinn, were approached in Arwenack Street, Falmouth, by a woman who reported that her husband had been brutally murdered. On investigation, the body of Albert Bateman was found bludgeoned to death in his tobacco shop (near the present site of Trago Mills). Nearby lay a gun whose bloody handle showed that it had been the implement used to beat the shopkeeper's brains out.

On checking its serial number it was found that the gun had been stolen from a ship at the docks. A dozen suspects were identified, among whom was one Gordon Horace Trenoweth. On Christmas Day police called on Trenoweth, and following his arrest it became clear that they had the right man. Fibres from his coat were found on the gun, and oil from it stained his pocket. He tried to convince officers that the blood on his jacket had resulted from a nose-bleed. But the clincher was a particular pound note, found in four pounds and ten shillings' worth of notes in Trenoweth's pocket.

The note in question had been meticulously repaired. Bateman, the victim, would often mend bank notes, and a piece of paper found in the shop's bin indicated that he had patched up the note earlier on the day that he succumbed to his untimely bludgeoning. Trenoweth was found guilty of murder, and on 6 April 1943, he was dangling by the neck at Exeter Prison.

THE BIGGEST SECRET
1944

1943 and 1944 saw American troops arrive in their thousands in Cornwall. Large camps were set up across the county in preparation for the D-Day landings. Groups such as the Truro-based 81st Tank Battalion (5th US Armored Division) were by no means idle during this time. Vehicles, weaponry and equipment were thoroughly checked over; there was plenty of maintenance work involving painting and greasing; light engineering, including modifications to tanks and armoured vehicles, engine rebuilds; and the assembly of trucks and trailers.

Cornwall contained tens of thousands of invasion troops based in small, well-camouflaged camps known as 'sausages' – secret marshalling areas – that were dispersed throughout the county. Planks were laid along well-trodden routes in the fields so that paths wouldn't be ground into the earth to be seen by the enemy from above. Any earth that was removed needed to be painted so that it blended in with the surrounding countryside.

Many of the US troop manoeuvres were held along the River Fal and the local beaches. A slipway was constructed at Grove Place for the use of landing craft and heavy transport – some of the concrete flagstones, looking like giant chocolate bars, can be seen behind the watersports clubhouse at Grove Place Boat Park.

On the eve of D-Day the troops and their equipment made their way along routes blocked to civilian traffic to a variety of places on the Cornish coast. Locals disturbed by the noise of troop movements on the night of 5 June woke to find no trace of the Americans. For example, Trebah beach saw the embarkation of 7,500 men from the 29th US Infantry Division (1st US Army). From here they crossed rough seas to set foot on Normandy. But most of the tanks with which they had so meticulously practiced in

Cornwall couldn't be landed with them as the carriers foundered and sank offshore. Their assault on German positions at Omaha Beach – the bloodiest of D-Day's five landing sites – cost a heavy price, as one in every three US troops fell as a casualty.

THE UBIQUITOUS CAMPERVAN
1947

Go into any gift shop in Cornwall and you're guaranteed to see two items in particular. The first is the St Piran's flag, a white cross upon a black background, a design that covers all manner of novelties and souvenirs, from real flags to mugs. The second item is a reproduction – be it in ceramics, plastic or metal – of the Volkswagen Type 2, known as the VW Camper in the UK. The vehicle, sometimes called the 'hippy van', can be seen absolutely everywhere in the county during the summer months in a fabulous array of conditions and colours, from beat-up old growlers more than half a century old to gleaming examples whose interiors haven't yet accumulated the sediment of ages.

The T2 is a panel van whose origin dates back to a doodle penned by Dutch businessman Ben Pon on 23 April 1947 (in case you're wondering, the T1 is the Volkswagen Beetle, whose origin can be traced to a 1932 doodle by a certain Adolf Hitler). The first T2 rolled off the Volkswagen production line in Germany on 12 November 1950, and since then it has undergone a few modifications and been transformed into a variety of 'official' incarnations, such as an ambulance version, a flatbed truck, and a semi-camping van; custom modifications are, of course, limitless. Enthusiasts often refer to the model by the number of windows – from the basic 11-window bus to the 23-window versions. You're likely to see a great range of T2 models on Cornwall's roads, including the more recent T2b 'breadloaf' with its single front bay windscreen (replacing the old split-screen of the older models), which was phased in from 1967 onwards. Sadly, it appears that production of the T2b will be ending in 2013.

Why is the T2 so popular in Cornwall? Undoubtedly it became an early favourite with surfers, having plenty of room inside and on top for wave-riding paraphernalia. Images of T2s in Cornwall can be found from the early 1950s onwards. The modern generation of surfers find that the T2 has ample space inside for the bodily contortions necessary for putting on and taking off a wetsuit. Although the link between surfers and hippies may seem obvious, it has always struck me that hippies are naturally shy of making any form of concerted physical effort, never mind if it helps a person commune with nature (as surfing does with a vengeance). Perhaps it's the long hair, but you rarely encounter a surfer with an extensive beard – it produces too much drag.

Even if you don't have a T2 but would like to live the Cornish dream, the county boasts more T2 hire centres than anywhere else in the UK. Failing that, you could always splash out in any gift shop and buy your own T2 souvenir.

AHARRR, JIM LAD!
1950

If for any reason you find the need to immerse yourself in the imagined world of 18th-century pirates, you may be tempted to conjure as a role model Jack Sparrow, as portrayed by Johnny Depp in the *Pirates of the Caribbean* movies. While the good (or is it bad?) Captain has a certain devilish charm, expressed in vague, semi-conscious piratical ramblings, he's not an eye-patch on your harsh, rough-and-ready Cornish pirate of which Long John Silver is a fine exemplar. Far nearer the genuine article, this salty character with a love of spitting sea-based obscenities through cutlass-gripping teeth is as familiar today as he was when he vividly burst like a broadside into the popular consciousness in 1950.

1950 was the year in which the movie *Treasure Island* was released – exactly a century after the birth of the story's writer, Robert Louis Stevenson. Stevenson had intended the book to be called *The Sea Cook*, but thankfully someone must have thought about potential sales. Who would want to read a novel outlining a sailor's galley-based culinary exploits? It turned out that the cook who emerged from Stevenson's vivid imagination was no ordinary character. The lynchpin of the story, Long John Silver is described as having no left leg 'and under the left shoulder he carried a crutch, which he managed with wonderful dexterity, hopping about upon it like a bird. He was very tall and strong, with a face as big as a ham – plain and pale, but intelligent and smiling'.

Silver's physical stature was based on Stevenson's friend William Henley, whom he described as 'a great, glowing, massive-shouldered fellow with a big red beard and a crutch; jovial, astoundingly clever, and with a laugh that rolled like music; he had an unimaginable fire and vitality; he swept one off one's feet'. While Stevenson doesn't specify Silver's place of origin, his manner of speaking has clear southwestern intonations.

Robert Newton (1905–56), one of Britain's leading movie stars of the 1940s and 1950s, was chosen to take the role of Long John Silver in the 1950 Disney adaptation of *Treasure Island*. Newton had starred in a wide variety of roles, from romance to high adventure; possessed of a 'Flynnesque' appeal, his young admirers included the morose comedian Tony Hancock, wild man actor Oliver Reed and legendary Who drummer Keith Moon. Newton played the role with relish, spicing up the character's voice with an exaggerated Cornish accent. So impressive was the performance that his accent formed the template from which all future portrayals of Silver – and pirates in general – was based. It's worth noting that Robert Newton was himself brought up in Cornwall, attending school in Lamorna, near Penzance. During the Second World War he served on HMS *Britomart* (named after the ancient Minoan goddess of hunting), which escorted Atlantic and Arctic convoys and was finally refitted in the southwest before being involved in the Normandy landings. After Newton's death in 1956 his ashes were scattered in the sea in Mount's Bay, off the coast from his old haunt at Lamorna. He may be long dead, but his pirate voice – along with plenty of brigand-based attitude – can be heard in modern cartoon favourites as varied as *SpongeBob SquarePants* (Patchy the Pirate) and *Family Guy* (the wooden-limbed Seamus the Pirate).

A SPELL IN THE MUSEUM
1960

For half a century Boscastle has been home to the Museum of Witchcraft. Claimed to be the largest collection of witchcraft-related artefacts and regalia in the world, the museum ranks among Cornwall's most popular attractions – for tourists with a taste for the macabre, that is.

The museum's founder Cecil Williamson (1909–99), a West Country man, had been interested in witchcraft since he was seven years old and had witnessed an elderly woman's public beating and stripping at the hands of a mob who had accused her of being a witch. In 1930, after spending time in Africa studying tribal magic, Williamson returned to England where he began to collect occult memorabilia. He also befriended a number of prominent occultists, including the horror writer Montague Summers and the self-styled 'Great Beast 666', Aleister Crowley. Williamson claimed to have used his knowledge of the occult before and during the Second World War to help MI6 in its attempts to thwart Nazi Germany. This may have been no fantasy, as it is well known that Britain employed a wide variety of measures to confound, confuse and divert the enemy, including consulting some unconventional characters who were capable of thinking 'out of the box'.

Williamson's first attempt to open a museum devoted to witchcraft in Stratford-upon-Avon in 1947 met with stiff local opposition and the project was never realised. Castletown on the Isle of Man became the location of his first museum, the Folklore Centre of Superstition and Witchcraft, which opened in 1949. In 1951 the Witchcraft Act of 1735 was finally repealed by Parliament, enabling Williamson to employ his friend Gerald Gardner as the resident witch. But there were bad vibes between the two and, following a breakdown of their partnership in 1952, Williamson took all of his exhibits back to England, where he re-established the museum at Windsor. Local opposition forced yet another wholesale move to the Cotswolds village of Bourton-in-the-Water in 1954. Six years later an arson attack forced the museum's final move to Boscastle, where it remains to this day. On Halloween in 1996 Williamson sold the museum to Graham King and Elizabeth Crow.

A remarkable collection of strange and unusual objects can be found at the Museum of Witchcraft. Charring from the arson attack of 1960 can still be seen on some of the exhibits, along with more recent damage caused by the great Boscastle flood of 2004 – the water's 'high tide' mark can be traced on the museum walls. Fortunately 90 per cent of the original exhibits were saved, and the museum underwent a renovation. Exhibits cover all aspects of the occult, and include: magical amulets; dolls used in curses; mandrakes and tiny mandrake coffins; healing herbs; a reconstruction of a 19th-century 'wise woman's' cottage; sculptures, images and writings on witchcraft; essential witchcraft equipment; Devil worship paraphernalia; scrying and divination artefacts; spells and charms. Although many of the exhibits are not directly linked with Cornwall, the (for now) final location of the museum in this strange county seems most appropriate.

EVERAGE OVER THE EDGE
1961

Comedic pratfalls are a much-loved and well-established part of British humour, and inadvertent falls from cliff edges have been a staple of cartoons and TV sketches for decades. Irony, a powerful component of humour, has also featured in real-life cliff accidents; for example, Jimi Heselden, owner of the Segway company and proud advocate of the safety of his two-wheeled transporters, died in 2010 when his own Segway veered off a cliff and plunged 215 feet.

Australian comedian Barry Humphries – better known to the public as his alter-ego Dame Edna Everage – was a rising star in 1961. Fresh to the UK and rapidly associating with leading members of the British comedy scene, Humphries very nearly failed to begin his rise to fame, and the glamorous 'suburban housewife from Melbourne' almost met her end only a few years after her inception. While on holiday with his wife at Zennor (a place that has long been associated with eccentric artists of one type or another), Humphries enjoyed taking strolls along the cliffs. One morning, while near the cliff edge, the 27-year-old Aussie funny-man lost his footing and fell backwards, tumbling 150 feet down a ravine to land on a narrow ledge high up on the cliff face. A filmed report of his rescue by helicopter subsequently featured on ITN news. Humphries may have broken a few bones in the fall, but thankfully the incident didn't damage his funny bone.

LIVE FROM THE STATES
1962

For more than a century, beginning with the work of Marconi, Goonhilly Downs on the Lizard served as a base for pioneering radio research and communications. It was here, on 23 July 1962, that one of broadcasting's greatest achievements was accomplished – the first live public television broadcast from the United States to the UK via satellite.

Work on Goonhilly earth satellite station was begun by the GPO (the General Post Office, who at the time were responsible for telecommunications in the UK). Its first big radio dish, Antenna 1 – affectionately known as Arthur – measured 85 feet across, weighed more than a thousand tons and cost £650,000. Goonhilly was the perfect choice for its location – the ground was flat, with clear views around the horizon, and the rock surface could easily bear Arthur's substantial weight.

Arthur was ready by the time NASA launched Telstar 1 (the first privately funded space mission) from Cape Canaveral on 10 July 1962. Unlike today's communication satellites, it assumed an elliptical orbit around the Earth inclined by 45 degrees to the equator, completing an orbit once every 2 hours and 37 minutes, ranging between a height of 592 and 3,687 miles. This placed a 20 minute per orbit limitation on Telstar's availability to relay transatlantic signals.

Arthur had a tracking accuracy of a minute fraction of a degree as it followed Telstar across the sky. After preliminary trials, TV signals from America's CBS and NBC networks were broadcast on the BBC in a joint show hosted by Walter Cronkite and Chet Huntley in New York, and the BBC's Richard Dimbleby in Brussels. Following the first pictures beamed from Andover in the USA – New York's Statue of Liberty and the Eiffel Tower in Paris

– the first action shown featured a televised game between the Philadelphia Phillies and the Chicago Cubs at Wrigley Field. It was to have featured a speech by President John F. Kennedy, but the signal was acquired before the President was ready.

At first, Arthur only had to deal with one television channel or 500 simultaneous telephone calls relayed by Telstar. But as more satellites filled Earth orbit, Goonhilly grew to 160 acres containing more than 60 dishes, which handled all manner of transmissions, from high-speed Internet data, TV signals and about 10 million telephone calls each week. Operations at Goonhilly ceased in 2008, but its dishes remain – they can easily be spotted on the horizon from high ground in mid-Cornwall. There is talk about opening the site as an active science centre, including using the dishes for radio astronomy.

STARGAZY PIE IS LIT UP
1963

Merry place you may believe,
Tiz Mouzel 'pon Tom Bawcock's eve
To be there then who wouldn't wesh, to sup o' sibm soorts
    o' fish
When morgy brath had cleared the path,
Comed lances for a fry
And then us had a bit o' scad an' Starry-gazie pie
As aich we'd clunk,
E's health we drunk, in bumpers bremmen high,
And when up came Tom Bawcock's name,
We'd prais'd 'un to the sky.

Traditionally sung to the tune of a wedding march in the fishing village of Mousehole in western Cornwall, the above verses are part of the celebration of Tom Bawcock's Eve on 23 December.

Bawcock is said to have been a local fisherman who lived in the 16th century. One particular winter had been extremely bad, with a succession of storms that had for many weeks prevented the fishing boats from leaving the harbour. Reliant on fish as an essential part of their diet, the villagers were facing a gloomy Christmas and the possibility of starvation. On 23 December, Tom Bawcock took it upon himself to take his fishing boat out, braving the storms and the atrocious seas. He returned with a catch ample enough to feed the entire village. Seven types of fish were baked in pies which were consumed by the hungry villagers – to prove that the pies contained fish, their heads were arranged to poke out of the crust.

Stargazy pie, as this dish became known, is eaten every year at the Festival of Tom Bawcock's Eve in Mousehole. Since 1963, the festival has been held beneath the Mousehole village illuminations, a display that lights up the village and entire harbour; there's even a large illuminated display representing a stargazy pie. During the parade, the villagers accompany a giant-sized stargazy pie through the streets during the evening, holding handmade lanterns, and then consume the pie itself. There's no evidence that Bawcock actually existed, nor that the village, facing certain starvation, was ever saved by one man's daring trawl. The celebration harkens back to an older feast, held towards the end of each year, when a pie was baked containing different fish that represented the variety of seafood the fishermen hoped to snag in the year to come.

A BIRDSEYE VIEW
1967

Surely, the most recognised sea captain after Captain Cook is the old sea-salt Captain Birdseye. Market research conducted in the 1970s revealed that most people saw this enthusiastic vendor of fish fingers as being a Cornishman, hearing in his gnarled but friendly voice the unmistakeable timbre of the West Country. He had the right look – a white, medium-length beard masking a cheery visage (possibly emanating a hint of last night's tot of rum) and slightly worn naval costume – a look that can be seen in many a Cornish fishing port to this day. But appearances can be deceptive.

Captain Birdseye was created in 1967 by Australian ad-man Dave Broad, who, only days away from Birds Eye's deadline and desperate for inspiration, flicked through a *Superman* comic. A train of thought ran through his mind: Superman ... Super sailor ... Captain Marvel ... Captain Birdseye.

The TV advertising role of Captain Birdseye was played by actor John Hewer, who was born in London. His depiction of the captain, which lasted between 1967 and 1998 (Hewer ageing from 45 to 76), included a distinctive West Country accent. It was a great choice, and the campaign proved immensely popular over the decades. Cornish Stoneware issued a Captain Birdseye fish-finger anniversary mug featuring Hewer's image, celebrating '30 yummy years' from 1955 to 1985 – the captain had been at the helm of the clipper for just 18 of those years.

In 1971 Birds Eye made the mistake of 'killing off' the good captain, announcing in an 'obituary' published in *The Times*: 'Birdseye, Captain. On June 7th, 1971, after long exposure, life just slipped through his fingers. Celebrity and gourmet. Mourned by Sea-Cook Jim and the Commodore, in recognition of his selfless devotion to the nutritional needs of the nation's children'.

Falling sales against ice-stiff competition amid the 'Cod War' forced Birds Eye to resurrect the character only three years later. Hewer's fingers were eventually loosened from the wheel when Captain Birdseye underwent a makeover in 1997. The 76-year-old was replaced for a while by Thomas Pescod, 31, whose image was that of a virile, dark-haired, stubble-chinned young adventurer. Keeping to character and with tongue in cheek, Hewer said: 'I'm glad to be handing over to an able captain. I've passed on all my nautical knowledge and skills. Now I'm going to spend the rest of my time on the coast of Cornwall to be near my friends and relatives.'

The younger Captain Birdseye portrayed by Pescod (an apt name if ever there was one) proved unpopular, and he was dropped to bring back the white-bearded original. This time he was played by Hewer lookalike (but much younger) Martyn Reid. Hewer died in 2008, two years before Captain Birdseye was dropped again in favour of a new icon – the laconic, freezer-dwelling Clarence the polar bear.

A FLAP OF FLYING CRYPTIDS
1976

Cornwall has its fair share of cryptozoological entities – highly elusive creatures that appear to shrug off attempts to pin down and place them in any recognised zoological category. One of the strangest cryptids reported in recent times is a creature known as Owlman – a winged, feathered, flying 'humanoid' with an owl-like face and large, piercing red eyes. It's the stuff of comic books. For decades it's also been the stuff of numerous serious articles and the subject of several books of purported non-fiction.

Owlman's story begins on 17 April 1976, when June and Vicky Melling (aged 12 and 9 respectively) reported being frightened by the sight of a feathered 'bird man' hovering over St Maunanus Church, a building in Mawnan that overlooks the cliffs on the Helford Estuary. On hearing the story and appreciating the genuine fear expressed by his daughters, Don Melling decided to cut the family holiday short and return to Lancaster.

On 3 July, Sally Chapman and Barbara Perry (both 14) were camping in the same woods near Mawnan where Vicky and June had reported Owlman (their courage must be applauded, since they were already aware of the earlier sighting). The teenagers' encounter was to be rather more up-close, personal and terrifying. That evening they were confronted by what, according to Chapman, looked like 'a big owl with pointed ears, as big as a man. The eyes were red and glowing. At first, I thought that it was someone dressed up, playing a joke, trying to scare us. I laughed at it, we both did, then it went up in the air and we both screamed.' On shooting up into the trees, the creature displayed black, pincer-like claws.

This is the general description that can be applied to most subsequent sightings of Owlman, as reported by various witnesses and paranormal investigators, notably long-time resident of Cornwall

Tony 'Doc' Shiels. The years 1978, 1979, 1989 and 1995 were 'flap' years for Owlman reports in the same area. Interestingly, most of the eyewitnesses have been young women.

Cryptozoologist Karl Shuker ventured that most of the reports are suggestive of a large owl. Having seen many birds of prey at large in Cornwall, and being all too familiar with nocturnal hoots and occasional low-level, soaring raptors, it's obvious that this would have to be an unusually large owl. Factoring in the reliability of witnesses to estimate size accurately, an escaped eagle owl or great grey owl might fit the bill – these majestic creatures can exceed 40 inches in height. Otherwise, we're faced with entertaining the notion of there being at large a humanoid of unknown origin with an inexplicable fondness for freaking people out.

A RADIOACTIVE COUNTY

1987

Planet Earth is made of rocks, and since all rocks have a natural level of radioactivity, everywhere on the planet experiences a degree of natural radiation. To a lesser extent we also receive natural radiation from space in the form of cosmic rays. Whatever its source, radiation has the same effects on biology, having the potential to destroy cells and to cause mutations in DNA. Life on Earth has evolved to cope with this by having cells with mechanisms of self-repair to any damage inflicted by these forms of natural radiation.

Levels of natural radiation vary considerably around the UK, with lows across Wales and the Midlands, while there are significant concentrated 'hotspots' in eastern Scotland, Devon and Cornwall. What makes these hotspots so radioactive is the nature of the rock – granite, an igneous rock formed deep inside the Earth that has intruded into overlying rocks like giant rising bubbles in a lava lamp. Some granites contain significant amounts of uranium, a substance that releases radioactive radon gas. Radon – invisible and without odour – poses a potential health problem in places where it can be trapped in pockets of air, such as down mineshafts and in deep basements and cellars. The risks of radon have only become clear since the mid-1980s, and the National Radiological Protection Board have been monitoring levels since 1987.

On average a person in the UK will receive around half of their annual dose of radiation from radon gas, 10 per cent from terrestrial rocks, 10 per cent from cosmic rays and the rest from artificial radiation sources including medical treatments and certain consumer products. That vintage watch with the luminous dials may not be as innocent as it looks! If you're ever out on the rocks in Cornwall, you can be sure of encountering many significantly radioactive rocks – but you wouldn't know it without a Geiger counter.

Around one in a hundred Cornish households have levels of radon seven times higher than the UK average; some houses have been found to have as much as twenty times the UK average. This is worrying, as radon is second only to smoking as a cause of lung cancer and kills 1,000 people annually in the UK. Someone living in an untreated basement in a high-radon house would experience the same cancer risks as if they were smoking a hundred packs of cigarettes a day! Measures can be (and have been) taken to reduce the risk, including free radon monitors and, if a risk is discovered, building work of one kind or another. There's nothing that can be done to change the nature of the rocks themselves – give it a few billion years and the problem will sort itself out by natural decay.

THE UFO FLAP THAT
TURNED INTO A FLOP
1993

In the small hours of 31 March 1993 hundreds of people who happened to be out and about in western parts of the UK, from the Midlands all they way down to Devon and Cornwall, reported seeing a large triangular-shaped craft (perhaps more than one) zipping across the night sky. That's the widely recounted story, anyway. A recently declassified report from the Ministry of Defence, originally compiled by Nick Pope shortly after the incident, states: 'It seems that an unidentified object of unknown origin was operating in the UK Air Defence Region without being detected on radar; this would appear to be of considerable defence significance, and I recommend that we investigate further, within MoD or with the US authorities'.

Pope was then working for a section of Secretariat (Air Staff), where his duties included investigating reports of UFO sightings in order to assess their potential defence significance. His boss, usually sceptical about the UFO phenomenon, agreed with Pope's conclusion, and in a brief to the Assistant Chief of the Air Staff wrote: 'In summary, there would seem to be some evidence on this occasion that an unidentified object (or objects) of unknown origin was operating over the UK.'

What exactly was observed? At 1 a.m. an MoD police patrol at RAF Cosford in Shropshire alerted the meteorological officer at nearby RAF Shawbury that an unusual object was approaching. The latter reported seeing vast triangular craft, accompanied by a low-pitched humming noise, which intermittently emitted a narrow, ground-sweeping beam of light. Later sightings of bright lights in the sky took place across the UK, most of them from Devon and

Cornwall between 1.10 a.m. and 1.15, but also from across northern France at around that time.

Further investigation revealed that the booster that had launched Russia's Cosmos 2238 radio satellite into orbit on the previous evening had re-entered Earth's atmosphere at around 1.10 a.m. along a path that took it directly over Cornwall and France. An atmospheric burn-up of space debris is a dramatic sight; most people have never seen a fireball breaking up at the edge of space. The case seemed pretty much 'open and shut', yet it remained argued against by Pope, who held out that the humming noise and strange probing lights reported by Shawbury couldn't be explained. In 2005 the MoD met man put the story straight. His sighting took place at 2.40 a.m., an hour and a half *after* the rocket's re-entry. And he was quite clear – the 'triangular-shaped UFO was later found to have been nothing more exotic than the Dyfed-Powys police helicopter following a stolen car down the A5 with its searchlight'.

Pope quit the MoD in 2006 to become a well-known fixture of the UFO scene, choosing to continue to promote the 'Cosford Incident' in talks and writing. The so-called 'case' has become so well established in UFO circles that the simple truth refuses to be acknowledged by those who 'want to believe' – making it hard to imagine what, if anything, would constitute evidence against ET or 'black ops'.

THE BEAST OF BODMIN

1995

Occupying 80 square miles of eastern Cornwall, Bodmin Moor is bleak and foreboding. Its grey bones of granite project above the earth here and there, likened by novelist Daphne du Maurier to 'giant furniture, with monstrous chairs and twisted tables'. This expanse of moorland with its own peculiar air of mystery is the perfect setting for the legend of a phantom creature, an elusive 'alien big cat' with a penchant for ripping livestock to pieces. Much like Arthur Conan Doyle's fictional Dartmoor monster, the Hound of the Baskervilles, the Beast of Bodmin sends shivers down the spine of many who venture out and about on the moor.

The very words 'Beast of Bodmin' have more hair-curling connotations than any other of the several English 'big cats in the wild', and for good reason. Given the preponderance of cattle mutilations, an official investigation into the matter was conducted by the Ministry of Agriculture, Fisheries and Food (MAFF) in 1995. While no verifiable evidence of 'big cats' of an exotic nature being at large in the countryside could be found after their six-month investigation, MAFF made no attempt to dismiss the notion completely.

Eyewitness accounts of a hefty black panther-like creature at loose on Bodmin Moor are plentiful – there are even a number of grainy images purporting to show it – but hard evidence has been in short supply. Soon after MAFF's announcement a skull was discovered near the River Fowey at the edge of the moor by 14-year-old Barney Lanyon-Jones and his brothers. Measuring four by seven inches and set with razor-sharp two-inch-long canines, the skull (missing its lower jaw) was identified as that of a young male leopard. However, since the bone showed signs of mechanical scraping and the back of the skull was truncated it was concluded that it had once been mounted in a leopard-skin rug!

In 1997 a set of pawprints found in mud by hikers on Bodmin were identified by Newquay Zoo experts as being fresh tracks made by an adult puma. A year later, a short piece of video footage appeared to show a similar animal; it was taken so seriously that an intensive search was undertaken involving police and the Armed Forces. Squadron Leader Andrew McCombe of 2625 County of Cornwall Squadron reported that although low cloud and mist had prevented a visual identification, infrared intruder-detection devices had been triggered during the night, indicating that something large had been moving along the same track where the video had been shot.

Since then the Bodmin area has seen occasional spates of apparently animal-caused cattle mutilations – sheep and calves being the most susceptible to attack. One farm near Cardinham reports having lost 14 sheep to mystery killings since 1998. Meanwhile, although no person has ever been harmed, the eyewitness reports and indistinct photographs keep accumulating.

A PRINCELY SUM
2000

With its unique legal status, Cornwall used to be classed with foreign countries for taxation purposes and was liable to double tax. This system was ended in 1838 with the Tin Duties Act, replacing it with an annual payment to the Duke of Cornwall (currently Prince Charles) to compensate for this loss of revenue (in addition to compensating the officers who collected the tax). The compensation of £16,216 was received by successive Dukes of Cornwall until 1983, when the Act was repealed by the Miscellaneous Financial Provisions Act 1983.

The repeal makes it theoretically legal for a separate Cornish tax to be levied by the Duke under the provisions of the Charter of the Duchy of Cornwall, although any revenue gained would be the revenue of the Duchy, not Prince Charles.

On 15 May 2000 an invoice for £20,067,900,000 (more than £20 billion) was received by the chief officer of the Duchy of Cornwall, the Lord Warden of the Stannaries. Sent by the 'Revived Cornish Stannary Parliament' (a pressure group formed in 1974), the invoice demanded a refund of a calculated overcharge by 100 per cent in taxation on tin production from 1337 (the birth of the Duchy) to 1837 (just before the Tin Duties Act came into force). Cornwall had been charged at over twice the rate levied on tin mining in Devon. The pressure group's stated aim was to use the money to revive the county's economy. However, the Duke of Cornwall, Prince Charles, serves as a trustee; since he is not permitted to sell the Duchy's assets he simply wouldn't be able to pay the bill!

EXRUPINATION MANIA
2003

Before continuing, it's best to point out that 'exrupination' is Latin for falling from a cliff. Most people would prefer not to perform such a seemingly suicidal action under any circumstances, but thrill-seekers and adrenaline junkies have managed to turn it into a kind of sport. Although it's the least inexpensive extreme sport to get into – all you need is a swimming costume, a suitably precipitous cliff to jump from and an adequate depth of water in which to splash – considerations of monetary cost alone will probably win it few converts.

Sunny Acapulco, set in a deep semicircular bay on the Pacific shore of Mexico, is the traditional home of the fearless cliff diver; for a century divers have plunged from the cliffs of La Quebrada, making it a popular attraction for tourists. Cliff-diving competitions are usually well-managed affairs at thoroughly researched venues, with skilled participants jumping from specially crafted platforms just clear of the cliff (or other precipice) in question.

While Cornwall isn't usually treated to the warm weather of Mexico, nor does it enjoy such pleasant sea temperatures, it has plenty of cliffs, and plenty of people willing to risk life and limb in pursuit of a temporary natural high and the adulation that participants earn by their expertise (or folly). And instead of organised cliff-diving, it has tombstoning, a high-risk practice, as its name suggests. It requires no special abilities other than to jump, fall and swim. Between 2006 and 2010 RNLI lifeboats responded to 98 tombstoning incidents on the coast, in which 58 people were rescued. Even the most carefully planned jump can go wrong because of misperceived water depth, submerged objects, hidden currents and the shock of plunging into cold water.

Coastal cliffs are not the only attraction for tombstoners, however. Cornwall has plenty of deep-sided, water-filled quarries that also fit the bill. Indeed, the UK's first known tombstoning fatality took place in 2003 when 24-year-old Stephen Royston jumped 100 feet into a quarry at Kit Hill, near Callington. In 2008, 28-year-old Steven Andrews broke his neck and was paralysed for life after a leap of just 20 feet off a cliff near Whitsand Bay.

Despite its risks, the craze shows no signs of abating. In July 2010 a 100ft 'leap of faith' from cliffs near Penzance by an unnamed tombstoner was captured on camera by Alastair Sopp, making local and national headlines and prompting many copycat leaps around the county. In 2012 twenty of Cornwall's top tombstoning sites were the recipients of official coastguard warning signs. In bold letters they proclaim, 'Don't jump in the water'. Most of us have no worries on that score.

A PARANORMAL
TRIP TO PENZANCE
2004

Cornwall's main road artery, the A30, follows a roughly east-west path, crossing the Devon border over the River Tamar, near the ancient town of Launceston. Since the age of the motor vehicle it has been the road most often travelled through the county.

Perhaps the true 'Beast of Bodmin' isn't a creature at all – it's the A30 itself, a road that has long been infamous for its horrendous traffic snarl-ups, particularly along the stretch between Bodmin and Indian Queens. So vital is the A30 to the life of Cornwall that the county's residents are just as much a prisoner to the whims of the fickle god of transport as are holidaymakers. Although it's true that road improvements have eased things since the 1990s, it's still not uncommon for motorists' eyes to be greeted by the disconcerting sight of a continuous, slow-moving, bumper-to-bumper line of cars, vans, caravans, campervans, trucks and lorries extending along the A30 as far as the eye can see. It's hardly surprising since an estimated 50,000 vehicles per day pass Bodmin during the summer – just one snag, however big or small, is capable of bringing things to a grinding halt.

On entering Cornwall the traveller is often struck by the rapid change in scenery, and those odd-sounding Cornish place names add to the perception of entering a dramatically different place. Before long you're traversing Bodmin Moor, where in places the road slices through solid granite. It was here in December 2006, near Temple, that the famous talkSPORT radio host Mike Dickin – a Bodmin man and Henry VIII lookalike, with some extreme and firmly-held views to boot – was involved in a fatal car crash. Strangely, Dickin had hosted shows that discussed the conspiracy theory of Princess Diana's car crash, and his very last show was about the afterlife and the existence of God (Dickin was an atheist, like his guest on the show, Richard Dawkins).

The western end of the A30 skirts Penzance and cuts across the Penwith promontory to Land's End. This section of the road, with its reports of phantom hitchhikers, makes it reputedly one of Cornwall's most haunted places. Such supernatural entities don't only exist in modern times: they crop up in centuries-old tales of phantoms terrorising unsuspecting horse-riders and passengers in horse-drawn coaches.

Some of the more recent paranormal links to the A30 concern motorists' sightings of UFOs, particularly from along those stretches of the road passing through rural areas that remain unlit at night. Flying saucers are no longer 'in'. The current trend seems to be weird-looking triangular or ring-shaped craft that are said to perform extraordinary manoeuvres at speeds unattainable by craft of terrestrial origin. According to *How to be Abducted by Aliens* (2004) one of the top places in the UK to see a UFO and experience a forced session in the company of extraterrestrials is the area surrounding Penzance (bear in mind that the booklet was published by the brewing company Grolsch to coincide with its alien-themed adverts). I recommend pulling into any convenient lay-by west of Buryas Bridge after sunset, where you stand a better chance of encountering any number of strange phenomena.

FLOOD WARNING
2004

Set within an area of outstanding natural beauty, the village of Boscastle on Cornwall's north coast is famed for a great many things. Its picturesque harbour, so loved by tourists, is compassed by sturdy stone walls constructed in 1584 by the legendary sea captain Sir Richard Grenville. As soon as the harbour is entered, the landscape either side steepens and narrows, giving the village itself precious little purchase on the land bordering the River Valency.

This seemingly innocent configuration of terrain acted as a devastating funnel for floodwaters on 16 August 2004, an event that caused extensive damage to buildings and injuries to many of Boscastle's 1,000-plus residents. It is estimated that half a billion gallons of water – a thousand Olympic-sized swimming pools' worth – cascaded through Boscastle during the course of the day. The sudden flood submerged roads beneath more than ten feet of water, swept 84 cars away (32 out to sea), washed away four footbridges and caused extensive damage to the famous Wellington Hotel. It prompted the UK's largest peacetime rescue operation in history, involving all but two of Cornwall's 31 fire brigade stations; 90 people were lifted to safety by seven military and coastguard helicopters.

Yet, astonishingly, nobody lost their life. Even more remarkable is the fact that the worst physical casualty was suffered by 85-year-old Vera Hancock, who after having been trapped for two hours in her flat by waters that rose up to her neck, broke her right thumb when the front door burst open under the pressure of the water (she later required an amputation of her finger and thumb).

This was by no means Boscastle's first deluge, nor was it to be the last. On 28 October 1827 resident Thomas Pope wrote:

One of the most awful days I ever experienced at Boscastle. It rained very heavily in the morning and whilst we were in the Chapel increasingly so – when about to leave the whole street was filled with a body of water rolling down and carrying all materials with it – that devastation and ruin were its concomitants. By about 1 o'clock the rain ceased leaving the fine McAdamised road in complete ruin, teams of wagon horses were saved with difficulty. Pigs belonging to the cottagers were taken off the roofs of houses. Mr Langford and the cottagers the west side of the bridge suffered much. But thro the goodness of God on the East River [Valency] the waters were raised but little and our property preserved in safety – I would mark the finger of divine providence and acknowledge his loving kindness.

Boscastle was subjected to floods by the same downpour-dealing deity in July 1847, September 1950, June 1957 and 1958, February 1963 and June 2007. Sadly, the village's geography means very little can be done to prevent flooding in the future, although some minor precautions have been taken, including the construction of a new culvert for the Valency.

HAUNTING BACKWAYS COVE
2008

Close to the golden beach of Trebarwith Strand on Cornwall's north coast lies Backways Cove, a beautiful rocky inlet that's pleasantly isolated, beyond the usual path taken by tourists. On fine days the place has a wonderful atmosphere, sunlight being reflected from behind by the angular cliffs on either side of the deep cove, lending the sea wonderful tints of deep blue.

In July 2008 I visited Backways Cove. Having done some prior research, I was fully aware of its reputation as a 'haunted' place. Apparently, paranormal activity had been reported there over a very long period of time, but for the most part reports were fairly non-specific and unimpressive, mainly featuring ghosts of drowned shipwrecked sailors. Another tale (with little provenance that I can find) describes how the disowned son of a local farmer took revenge on the brother who had inherited the estate by burning down the farm – only to find that his brother had died the previous day and had left the farm to him.

It's nice to have a little background information on any place one might visit, but I was pretty unimpressed by these tales. Paranormal investigation – even contemplation of the paranormal – is something that I'm happy to let other people do. The walk down to the cove was undemanding, and once there I chose a suitably flat rock upon which to sit and take some refreshment. It was a warm, sunny day with patchy, white fluffy cloud; a slight sea breeze wafted through the cove. Before long I decided to make a colour study of the place on my hand-held tablet computer, and after ten or fifteen minutes I'd completed the preliminary sketch. An island further out from the cove fascinated me, as it appeared to be slanting to the west, as if pushed by the winds. Immediately adjacent to this island, projecting from the sea, was a much smaller yellowish rock that contrasted with the main island's green hue; the rock appeared to be the remnants of a small natural arch that had collapsed, leaving a curved stack, shaped like a bent arm reaching for the island.

After moving on to the foreground detail of the cove my computer suddenly lost power; to my intense annoyance the battery had come loose and as a result my sketch was gone. Yet my annoyance was short-lived. While taking a little more refreshment I casually looked at the scene once again; I was struck by the fact that the little 'stack' near the island was no longer there. The tide could not possibly have raised by several metres to cover it, nor could I imagine that a pile of solid rock had collapsed without my notice.

On further investigation, it seems that the feature I thought I saw and sketched has never existed. To this day I am mystified – perhaps it was a tree trunk or some debris that had temporarily reared up next to the island after getting one end lodged under the sea? Or perhaps it was the ghostly arm of a shipwrecked sailor vainly attempting to cling to safety? Your guess is as good as mine.

A SPACEBIRD'S-EYE VIEW OF CORNWALL

2010

Orbiting 200 miles above the Earth, the International Space Station (ISS) passes over the UK four times a day, every day. On most occasions it goes over in broad daylight or when it's in the Earth's shadow, so on these occasions it can't be seen from the ground. It's only when the ISS passes over a spot within one or two hours of local sunrise or sunset, when it is lit by the sun and visible against a sufficiently dark sky background, that it can be seen as a bright, slowly moving starlike point from the ground. Appearances of the ISS occur in a general two-month cycle, where it's visible every evening for a fortnight, with a break of a fortnight, followed by a fortnight of morning appearances, then another break of a fortnight, the cycle then repeating.

However, Cornwall itself can be seen from the ISS during every one of the six-hourly flyovers – providing, of course, the weather is clear enough. If you're ever on board, make for the wonderful observation cupola – a bay containing seven of the largest windows ever flown in space, which was specially installed in 2010 for astronauts to gaze out of. The southwest peninsula, set against the azure of the Atlantic Ocean and the continental shelf, is a very prominent landmark as viewed from orbit. Hand-held camera images taken by astronauts on board show a tremendous amount of detail across Cornwall, particularly the browns and tans of the moors (Bodmin Moor being the largest), and the vast open china clay quarries of central Cornwall (which it would be possible to also discern from the moon). Cornwall's beautiful sandy beaches are also prominent, those bordering St Ives Bay being especially noticeable. Despite its relatively small size, St Michael's Mount, too, can be seen without any optical aid from the space station. You can even observe the bright wakes of larger vessels going to and from Cornwall's many ports.

Night-time views of Cornwall from space reveal the lights of scattered settlements, threaded together with a few of the main A-roads. The brightest lights are to be found in the central-west region, with dense illumination inland at Truro and Redruth, while coastal towns such as St Austell, Falmouth and Penzance outline the county's shape – the lights of Newquay are the most dazzling of all. Those vast open clay quarries that are illuminated by searchlight at night show up as intense white spots, while Bodmin Moor retains its mystery, appearing as a black, desolate, unlit expanse.

Images of Cornwall from space can easily be accessed from various NASA sites, including the place-searchable Gateway to Astronaut Photography of Earth (http://eol.jsc.nasa.gov).

A MYSTERY TSUNAMI
2011

On the morning of 29 June 2011 a tsunami made its way along the south coast of England, moving west from Portsmouth to Penzance. With a wave peak height of less than two feet, this was by no means a violent event, nor did it do any reported damage to property or individuals, but it was pretty unusual and made the headlines because it occurred only three months after the devastating tsunami in Japan. The Tidal Gauge Anomaly measure, which records the difference between the forecast tide and the actual tide, showed that the wave-anomaly was eight inches in Newlyn, ten in Penzance and twelve in Plymouth.

Scores of people at St Michael's Mount reported the unusual sensation of their hair standing on end (thought to have been caused by a lowering of air pressure) as water built up on the eastern side of the causeway, ten inches higher than on the western side, before covering it and forcing visitors caught on the causeway to rush for the shore or the Mount. Interviewed by the BBC, holidaymaker Ben Talbot said: 'It was typical Cornish weather, hot and a bit muggy. I was just about to start off over to St Michael's Mount when my head felt prickly and my hair started standing up. Then there was a kind of whoosh and the sea on the bay side literally lifted up and swamped the cobbled causeway. I think a couple got caught in it but I couldn't tell you where they are now – quite obviously they were OK – but they would have got soaked. It was definitely odd and pretty un-nerving. But I didn't see any of the traditional tsunami signs – like retreating water – so there wasn't any panic.'

While digging for bait on the shore at nearby Marazion, Simon Evans did notice the waters retreat before the wave hit. He said: 'It was really eerie. The weather was really foggy but extremely warm and close, and the sea was as calm as a millpond. One minute

I was stood at the water's edge then when I turned around the water had retreated around fifty yards. It was surreal. I couldn't believe what had happened and had no idea what caused it, but I didn't really want to hang about and find out. Having heard about tsunamis, I jumped in the car and got out of there.'

There was initial speculation that a landslide on the sea bed far off the coast had caused the anomalous wave, but the British Geological Survey later concluded, on the basis of seismic records, that this was unlikely. It was probably a 'meteotsunami' caused by freak weather conditions, a transient disturbance in air pressure that produces sudden, short-lived changes in local sea level.

CLIFFS OF DOOM
2011

Battered by the relentless action of the Atlantic Ocean (or the Celtic Sea, if you prefer a more local marine nomenclature) and more exposed to the driving elements of tide, wave and wind, Cornwall's northern coastline is of a wilder, more rugged nature than the south.

Cornwall's cliffs can be enjoyed along miles of coastal pathway. But whether you're atop the giddying heights of the north-coast cliffs, enjoying a stroll along those more vertically challenged precipices in the south – or even enjoying the neck-craning view from the beach below – it's worth bearing in mind that those danger signs are put there for a purpose. Although they may appear solid and sturdy enough to take everything that's thrown at them, the dynamic junction between land and sea, combined with freak weather and the force of gravity, causes dozens of sizeable cliff collapses along the coast every year. Some of these invariably involve both animal and human fatalities. One of the most notorious areas for tumbling cliffs is Deadman's Cove and Hell's Mouth in Gwithian, on the north coast, northeast of St Ives Bay. In October 2011 video footage of a dramatic cliff collapse involving 100,000 plummeting tons made national headlines; the cliff walker who captured the scene was incredibly lucky not to have been a few hundred yards further east when the event took place.

Let's look at a few interesting cliff-related cataclysmic statistics between the years 1900 and 2000 (compiled according to the best efforts of my own research). An annual average of around 80 sizeable cliff falls and landslips removes 2,400 square metres of coastal outline each year, including several individual buildings (most of which have been abandoned long in advance). Together, these events have shifted more than 10 million tons of rock over the course of a century – that's more than twice the weight of the Great Pyramid of Giza.

Among the many precipitous cliffs found in the north, the appropriately named High Cliff near Boscastle represents the highest, measuring 223m (732 feet) from its vertiginous edge to rocky base. At least 70 suspected suicides have been recorded over the past century from this one stretch of cliffs alone. Still, I suppose that's nothing compared with the annual suicide rate of 20 unfortunates from Beachy Head in East Sussex (despite Beachy Head being only two-thirds the height of High Cliff). Cornwall's southern coast, with its less severe but equally impressive scenery, is blessed with sheltered estuaries amid green hills that roll down to the shore; I haven't compared cliff-related self-destruction between north and south, but it's reasonable to speculate that it is less of a problem in the south.

While Cornwall's murder rate is slightly lower than the national average, its suicide rate is just a bit higher, and its cliffs figure as a common factor in a substantial number of these crimes and misadventures. Fatal falls from the county's high coast account for some 1.5 per cent of murders in the past decade and 2.7 per cent of suicides in the same period. That's something for every fan of Daphne du Maurier or W. J. Burley's *Wycliffe* to ponder.

CORNWALL'S NATIONAL DISH
2011

Pasties of various sorts have been part of British cuisine since the 13th century but it was only during the 18th century that tin and copper miners in Cornwall began to enjoy the traditional Cornish pasty – a complete meal of lightly peppered chunky beef skirt, potato, turnips and onions packaged in a handy, tasty, D-shaped pastry wrapper. The advantages of such a food are obvious. The Cornish pasty retains its heat well because pastry is an excellent insulator. Moreover, a decent purchase on the savoury dish could be had by dirty, mineral-contaminated hands grasping the thick crimped side edge of pastry – this bit, which could well contain arsenic from the mine after handling, could be thrown away.

Miners' wives often marked the pasties with their husband's initials or a special symbol at one end so they could be picked out of the warming ovens that were built at some mines. This may have resulted in the traditional way of eating a Cornish pasty – from one end to the other – saving that half of the meal with the mark so that it could be eaten later, without fear of polishing off someone else's half-eaten pasty.

Nearly 100 million examples of the national dish of Cornwall are eaten each year. In July 2011, the Cornish pasty was awarded Protected Geographical Indication (PGI) status by the European Commission. To be called a Cornish pasty it must be prepared in Cornwall and have the ingredients and attributes as described above.

In Bodmin in August 2010, the 'Proper Cornish' bakers made the largest Cornish pasty in history. Around 15 feet long and weighing 1,900lb, it contained 360lb of beef, 180lb of turnips, 100lb of spuds and 75lb of onions. Costing £7,000 to make, the giant meal contained an estimated 1.75 million calories. After being cooked for 11 hours, it was broken up and eaten by the assembled crowd.

Tin miners in Cornwall were, perhaps unsurprisingly, of a superstitious nature. They believed in spirits called 'knockers', so-called because they produced a knocking sound that either guided the workers to undiscovered veins of ore or warned of an impending catastrophe such as a tunnel collapse. Respectful of these spirits, miners customarily left the knockers a part of their pasty in the mine for them to eat. Sailors and fishermen around Cornwall, however, believed that it was bad luck to bring a pasty aboard.

In Cornwall you may see the word 'oggy' on pasty shops and bakers. The word comes from 'hogen', the Cornish word for pasty. It's said that the miners would know when their pasties were ready for eating when the words 'Oggy, Oggy, Oggy' were shouted down from above, to which the miners would respond 'Oi, Oi, Oi!'.

An old Cornish proverb told of the Devil's refusal to enter Cornwall for fear of ending up as a filling in a pasty. Though Satan's flesh never ended up in a pasty, the dish has certainly had a wide variety of unofficial fillings over the centuries. A playground-rhyme of the 1940s went as follows:

Matthew, Mark, Luke and John, ate a pasty five feet long,
Bit it once, bit it twice, Oh my Lord, it's full of mice.

At the time of publication, since the Cornish pasty received its rightful recognition in law, horsemeat has never been found in one yet!

CORNWALL'S
EXPANDED COSMOS
2012

It's a little-known fact that much more of the universe can be seen from Cornwall than anywhere else in the UK. This is not based upon the pleasant fact that the county's skies are far darker on the whole than many parts of the UK, especially when compared to the orange-tinted light-polluted miasma over the urban sprawls of London, the Midlands and the Northwest. No, being the most southerly county, Cornwall has a southern horizon that opens up onto more southerly celestial realms than the rest of the UK.

Cornwall's most southerly point, the Lizard, is located at a latitude of 50 degrees north; London is at 52 degrees, York is 54 degrees and John O' Groats in Scotland is almost 59 degrees north. This means that the Pole Star is nine degrees higher in the sky at John O' Groats than at the Lizard – and it also means that the most southerly stars you can see from the Lizard are nine degrees below the horizon at John O' Groats. That might not sound much but it's 18 times the width of the full moon.

During the course of a year the band of southerly sky on the celestial sphere that is revealed from the Lizard but not from John O' Groats measures 9 x 360 degrees – that's a staggering 3,240 square degrees, exactly one-twentieth of the area of the entire celestial sphere, equivalent to nearly three times the area of the constellation of Ursa Major (the Great Bear). This zone of extra Cornish sky contains around 300 naked-eye stars and 5 billion distant galaxies.

An amateur astronomer known to me (but who shall remain nameless) is so enamoured with the idea of delving into deep southerly skies from Cornwall that he frequently packs up his telescope and takes the train down from London to survey the skies from a cliff-top over the weekend. What can he see? Well, the constellations of Scorpius and Sagittarius, home to the centre of the galaxy, can be viewed in astonishing detail, their many bright star clusters and nebulae standing out prominently even through binoculars and small telescopes. One can virtually write these constellations off if you live in a big city, as they never clear the sky-glow on the horizon. Other constellations that poke their heads above the Cornish southern horizon include such entities as Vela (the Sails), Antlia (the Air Pump), Corona Australis (the Southern Crown), Lupus (the Wolf), Centaurus (the Centaur), Columba (the Dove), Caelum (the Chisel), Phoenix (the Phoenix), Grus (the Crane) and Microscopium (the Microscope). No, there really is a chisel and an air pump – these are all genuine, officially recognised star patterns, many of them having only received names when seafaring explorers ventured into the southern hemisphere in the 16th century and saw them in all their glory. Some imagination, though, is required to visualise them!

TSUNAMIS OF
THE FUTURE
c. 12,000

Geologists think that increasing pressure on the same fault off the coast of Portugal that caused the Lisbon earthquake of 1755 will – at some point in the future – cause another megathrust earthquake of the same magnitude. A study by the British Geological Survey and the Proudman Oceanographic Laboratory, commissioned in 2006 by Defra, examined in detail the possible effects of a tsunami caused by just such an occurrence.

The worst-case scenario saw the generation of a tsunami that would take around five hours to reach Cornwall, causing sea levels at Mount's Bay to rise by twelve feet, with maximum wave heights of ten to twenty feet around the rest of Cornwall. This would produce severe damage to coastal areas in the UK, especially those of Cornwall, with waves travelling further inland and increasing in height as they were funnelled up the county's many estuaries and river valleys. Depending on the regular tidal situation, Truro city centre would stand a chance of being flooded as the wave progressed.

Apart from a sub-marine earthquake, undersea landslide, meteo-tsunami or asteroid impact, a tsunami affecting Cornwall could also be generated by the eruption of the unstable Cumbre Vieja volcano in La Palma on the Canary Islands and the subsequent landslide of half the mountain into the Atlantic. This possibility is clear from geological evidence, and out of all the UK Cornwall stands to bear the brunt of such a tsunami. It is estimated that the waves would take around six hours to reach Cornwall, reaching peak heights of up to 30 feet. Needless to say, these are pretty scary claims, and there is no way of telling how accurate these computer-modelled predictions are. Some geologists think that Cumbre Vieja is far more stable than is widely believed, estimating that the dangers won't be significant for another 10,000 years or more, so you don't need to think about cancelling that Cornish holiday just yet.

CUSTOMS AND EXERCISE
ANNUALLY

Out of a very large field of curious Cornish customs, many of whose origins date to a time before records began, two in particular stand out for their very oppositeness – Hurling the Silver Ball at St Columb Major (Easter) and the 'Obby 'Oss festival at Padstow (May Day)

Hurling the Silver Ball is an ancient outdoor team game unique to Cornwall, once played all over the county. The game is held once on Shrove Tuesday and again 11 days later. Play begins in the Market Square when a 10lb silver ball is tossed by the previous winner into the gathered players (usually around 50 in number) representing either town or country team. In what looks like a free-for-all melee (but with participants usually having fun), the objective is for an individual to score a single goal by taking it over the parish boundary or to a set goal point either at Tregamere Turn (a mile northeast of the town) or Cross Putty junction (a mile to the southwest of the town centre). No area is off-limits, and fields, streets, gardens and other property (sometimes houses) are often invaded by pursued and pursuers. With an area of 20 square miles, the parish of St. Columb Major is the largest pitch for any ball game in the world!

After midnight at the beginning of each May there can be heard singing around the Golden Lion Inn, Padstow. The chants (at least the majority of them) aren't drink-fuelled, nor are the musical strains of a familiar modern chord. When morning comes luscious greenery, flowers and flags have appeared to cover the town, and a maypole has been erected. Festivities begin at 10 a.m. when two 'osses, one red and the other blue, emerge from their respective 'stables'; each 'oss is controlled by one person dressed in a stylized representation of a horse with a pretty scary mask. Led by a Teazer and accompanied by groups of dancers and musicians, the procession makes its way through the streets, followed by the gathered crowds singing the traditional May song, a hypnotic tune sung to the beat of drums. Likely dating back more than 1,500 years, the 'Obby 'Oss festival at Padstow may have its roots in the ancient Celtic worship of horse deities.

BIBLIOGRAPHY

AA. *Leisure Guide Cornwall* (AA Publishing, 2011).

Acton, Viv. *Operation Cornwall, 1940–44: the Fal, the Helford and D-Day* (Landfall, 1994).

Allen, Judy. *The Encyclopedia of the Unexplained: Curious Phenomena, Strange Superstitions and Ancient Mysteries* (Kingfisher, 2006).

Berresford Ellis, Peter. *The Cornish Saints* (Tor Mark, 1998).

Bird, Sheila. *Cornish Tales of Mystery and Murder* (Countryside Books, 2002).

Bottrell, William. *Traditions and Hearth-side Stories of West Cornwall* (Bottrell, 1870).

Bottrell, William. *Stories and Folk-Lore of West Cornwall* (Bottrell, 1890).

Brown, H. Miles. *Battles Royal: Charles I and the Civil War in Cornwall* (Libra, 1982).

Clegg, David. *Cornwall and the Isles of Scilly: A Complete Guide* (Matador, 2005).

Collins, Wilkie. *Rambles Beyond Railways; or, Notes in Cornwall Taken A-Foot* (Bentley, 1851).

Cooke, Ian. *Journey to the Stones: Mermaid to Merrymaid – Ancient Sites and Pagan Mysteries of Celtic Cornwall* (Men-an-Tol Studio, 1996).

Coulson-Thomas, Colin. *Cornwall's Conquest of the Air -- the Fascinating Facts, from Marconi to Goonhilly* (Heritage, 1975).

Davison, Brian. *Tintagel Castle* (English Heritage, 2000).

Downes, Jonathan. *The Owlman and Others* (CFZ Press, 2006).

Drew, Samuel. *Immateriality and the Immortality of the Soul* (Essay, 1802).

Dunmore, Helen. *Zennor in Darkness* (Penguin, 1993).

Embrey, P.G / Symes, R.F. *Minerals of Cornwall and Devon* (TSO, 1987).

Fort, Charles. *The Complete Books of Charles Fort* (Dover, 1975).

Gary, Gemma. *Traditional Witchcraft: A Cornish Book of Ways* (Troy, 2008).

Gibson, James (Ed). *Thomas Hardy: The Complete Poems* (Palgrave, 2001).

Goldsmith, R.F.K. *Duke of Cornwall's Light Infantry* (Leo Cooper, 1970).

Gosse, Philip. *The History of Piracy* (Tudor, 1934).

Grolsch. *How to be Abducted by Aliens* (Grolsch, 2004).

Halliday, F.E. *A History of Cornwall* (House of Stratus, 2008).

Hamilton Jenkin, A.K. *Cornwall and its People* (David & Charles, 1988).

Hancock, Peter. *Cornwall at War, 1939-45* (Halsgrove, 2009).

Harrison, Paul. *Sea Serpents and lake Monsters of the British Isles* (Robert Hale, 2002).

Hunt, R. (Ed). *Popular Romances of the West of England* (Chatto and Windus, 1903).

Jones, Harold Spencer. *John Couch Adams and the Discovery of Neptune* (Cambridge University Press, 1947).

Jones, Kelvin (Ed). *Folklore and Witchcraft of the Cornish Village* (Oakmagic, 2004).

Kaczynski, Richard. *Perdurabo: The Life of Aleister Crowley* (North Atlantic Books, 2010).

Lawrence, D.H. *Kangaroo* (Secker, 1923).

Malory, Thomas. *Le Mort d'Arthur* (Caxton, 1471).

Marnham, Patrick. *Wild Mary: the Life of Mary Wesley* (Vintage, 2007).

Merrick, Hettie. *The Pasty Book* (Tor Mark, 1995).

Mudd, David. *The Cruel Cornish Sea* (Bossiney, 1981).

Mustill, Julia. *Summer Needs No Brightening: An Gof and the 1497 Cornish Rebellion* (Blue Elvan, 1997).

Newman, Paul. *Haunted Cornwall* (Tempus, 2005).

Noall, Cyril. *Cornish Shipwrecks* (Tor Mark, 1981).

Oldfather, C. H. (Translator). *Library of History: Loeb Classical Library* (Harvard University Press, 1935).

Parker, Bruce. *The Power of the Sea: Tsunamis, Storm Surges, Rogue Waves and Our Quest to Predict Disasters* (Mac-Sci, 2010).

Payton, Philip. *Cornwall: A History* (Cornwall Editions, 2004).

Payton, Philip. *The Cornish Overseas* (Cornwall Editions, 2005).

Petrie, Francis. *Roll Out the Barrel: the Story of Niagara's Daredevils* (Boston Mills, 1985).

Pope, Nick. *Open Skies, Closed Minds* (Simon & Schuster, 1996).

Ratcliff, Nora (Ed). *The Journal Of John Wesley* (Nelson, 1940).

Reader's Digest (Ed). *Folklore, Myths and Legends of Britain* (Reader's Digest, 1973).

Rowe, David. *Boscastle: 16th August 2004 – The Day of the Flood* (Truran, 2006).

_____

Rowe, Toni-Maree. *Cornwall in Prehistory* (The History Press, 2005).

Salmon, Arthur. *The Cornwall Coast (Unwin*, 1910).

Semmens, Jason. *The Cornish Witch-finder: William Henry Paynter and the Witchery, Ghosts, Charms and Folklore of Cornwall* (Federation of Old Cornwall Societies, 2008).

The Times (Ed). *The Times Britain From Space* (Times Books, 2000).

Tregellas, Walter Hawken. *Cornish Worthies: Sketches of Some Eminent Cornish Men and Families* (Stock, 1884).

Turner, Mike. *Clay Country Voices* (The History Press, 2000).

Underwood, Peter. *Ghosts of Cornwall* (Bossiney, 1998).

Van der Kiste, *John/Sly, Nicola. Cornish Murders* (The History Press, 2007).

Vivian, John. *Tales of the Cornish Smugglers* (Tor Mark, 2001).

Weatherhill, Craig. *A Concise Dictionary of Cornish Place-names* (Evertype, 2009).

Wesley, Mary. *The Camomile Lawn* (Macmillan, 1984).

White, Paul. *Ancient Cornwall* (Tor Mark, 2000).

ACKNOWLEDGEMENTS

To my Aunt Pat, lover of Cornwall.

My sincere thanks to Malcolm Croft, Commissioning Editor at Portico, for having entrusted me with writing *Cornwall's Strangest Tales* and for his tremendous support during its writing. Tina and Jacy, my wife and daughter, have also been very supportive, and both are now keen to explore with me the many strange places written about in this book.

My research was helped by the many friendly staff of the library services of both Cornwall and Plymouth, along with innumerable guides and staff at a variety of venues around Cornwall who have been willing to answer a question or two.

Finally, thanks to Empoleon and Accelgor for their help in enabling me to write substantial chunks of this book from the comfort of the Eden Project Cafe in St Austell.

Created in 2007, Portico publishes a range
of books that are fresh, funny and forthright.

PORTICO

An imprint of **Anova** Books

PLEASE VISIT **WWW.ANOVABOOKS.COM** TO SEE
MORE FANTASTIC TITLES PUBLISHED BY PORTICO

For your reading pleasure

THE
STRANGEST
SERIES

The *Strangest* Series has been delighting
and enthralling readers for decades with
weird, exotic, spooky and baffling tales of
the absurd, ridiculous and the bizarre.
This bestselling range of fascinating books
– from the Ashes to Fishing, Football to
London and Motor Racing to the World Cup,
detail the very curious history of each subject
area's funniest, oddest and most compelling
characters, locations and events.
For all things weird and wonderful, pick
up a *Strangest* from Portico Books today…

9781861052933

9781861055354

9781861052926

9781861051844

9781905798162

9781861054111

9781861057457

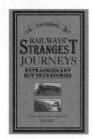

9781861056795

9781907554339

9781907554971

9781861059765

9781861058270

9781907554131

9781861059383

9781906032906

9781905798285

AND NOW FOR SOMETHING EVEN STRANGER!

9781906032760   9781906032913   9781907554476

The Strangest Series has now introduced even stranger
delights for its readers. With *The Ashes' Strangest*,
World Cup's Strangest and *Olympics' Strangest*,
fans of this unique and extraordinary series can delve
even deeper into the world of the bizarre and utterly
ridiculous with these special sport-related *Strangests*.
A great read no matter where you are, these fascinating
books highlight the bizarre, weird and downright bonkers
events, characters and locations of each particular sport.
Just don't read them all at once though – you might
start acting all peculiar! You have been warned.

IF YOU ENJOYED THIS PORTICO TITLE, YOU MIGHT ALSO ENJOY...

WROTTEN ENGLISH

A Celebration of Literary Misprints, Mistakes and Mishaps

Peter Haining

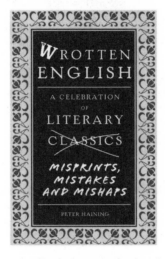

'An absolute gem of a book'
booksmonthly.co.uk

Following on from the hilarious collection of typos, gaffes and howlers in Portico's *A Steroid Hit the Earth*, comes *Wrotten English* – a fabulously funny collection of literary blunders from classic, and not-so classic, works of literature. This book is an anthology of side-splitting authors' errors, publishers' boobs, printers' devils, terrible titles, comical clangers and all manner of literary lunacy dating back since the invention of the printing press.

£9.99 • Hardback • 9781907554100

THE HIDDEN MATHEMATICS OF SPORT

Rob Eastaway & John Haigh

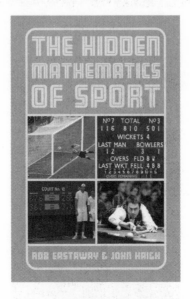

'A fascinating mixture of analysis, trivia and sporting history,
with plenty to appeal to any sports fan'

Ed Smith, *The Times*

The Hidden Mathematics of Sport takes a novel and intriguing look
at sport, by exploring the mathematics behind the action. Discover
the best tactics for taking a penalty, the pros and cons of being a
consistent golfer, the surprising link between boxing and figure
skating, the unusual location of England's earliest 'football' game
(in a parish church), and the formula for always winning a game of
tennis. Whatever your sporting interests, you will find plenty to
absorb and amuse you in this entertaining and unique book – and
maybe you will even find some new strategies for beating the odds.

£9.99 • Hardback • 9781907554223

WHATEVER HAPPENED TO TANGANYIKA?

The Place Names that History Left Behind

Harry Campbell

'Marvellous and intriguing, Campbell has created a whole new discipline – one which we may perhaps call nostalgic geography'

Alexander McCall Smith

In this fascinating trawl through the atlas of yesteryear, Harry Campbell explains how and why the names of countries, cities and counties have changed over time, and tells the extraordinary tales behind places from Rangoon to Rutland and Affpiddle to Zaire. *Whatever Happened to Tanganyika?* is a treasure trove of stories to delight armchair travellers and history fans alike.

£9.99 • Hardback • 9781906032050

365 REASONS TO BE CHEERFUL

Magical Moments to Cheer Up Miserable Sods ...
One Day at a Time

Richard Happer

It's a well-observed fact that human beings can be a grumpy old bunch, always choosing to see that infamous metaphorical glass as constantly half empty rather than half full. Where's the fun in that? *365 Reasons To Be Cheerful* is, well, it's exactly that. It's a whole year's worth of funny and unique events that happened on each and every day – a wild, weird and wonderful journey through the year highlighting the moments that changed the world for the better as well as the delightfully quirky stories that will simply make you smile. *365 Reasons To Be Cheerful* is designed specifically to look on the bright side of life every day of the year – the perfect pint-sized pick-me-up in these sobering, sombre times.

£7.99 • Hardback • 9781906032968